CUSTOMER SERVICE HANDBOOK

Valerie H. Lunden, M.A.

Monkey Mentors™

Customer Service Handbook

www.brightperformance.com

Book design: Jim Bisakowski www.bookdesign.ca

Library of Congress Cataloging-in-Publication Data available upon request.

Lunden, Valerie H.

Bright Performance Ltd.

ISBN – 978-0-9822539-1-5

Published in the United States of America

Dedication

To the brilliant and incomparable Gerard,
whom I met on that memorable plane ride a long time ago.

Contents

Introduction 1

Monkey See

Chapter One — Fairy-Tale Manufacturing 9

Chapter Two — Service-Bound Monkey 17

Chapter Three — Customer Types 23

Chapter Four — Trained to Push Buttons 33

Chapter Five — Beware of the Competition 39

Chapter Six — Monkey Migration 47

Chapter Seven — Continuous Civility 55

Chapter Eight — The Mission 61

Chapter Nine — The Tag Team 73

Monkey Say

Chapter Ten — Why the Customer Always Wins 81

Chapter Eleven — Service Templates: The Destroyers! . . 89

Chapter Twelve — You Are Going to Transfer Me Where? 95

Chapter Thirteen — Web Solutions? 105

Chapter Fourteen — Solutions in Motion 113

Monkey Do

Chapter Fifteen	Monkey Follow-Through	125
Chapter Sixteen	Gift Days	131
Chapter Seventeen	Business Responsiveness	135
Chapter Eighteen	The Best Team in Town	139
Chapter Nineteen	Cultural Divides	147
Chapter Twenty	Service Technology	153
Chapter Twenty-One	Important Versus Necessary	157
	Monkey Terms	161
	End Notes	162
	References & Notes	164
	Bibliography	168

Introduction

"The purpose of business is to create and keep a customer."
—Peter Drucker

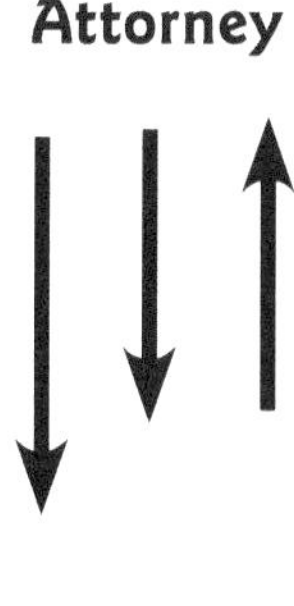

Superior customer service could be described as the creative actions of people. People doing their best and utilizing what they know to help others.

A memorable customer service experience I had involved my attorney; his name is John. I was introduced through a mutual friend who had spoken highly of John's competence; he was not only an attorney but also a CPA.

I had retained John's services to complete my will. I considered this a straightforward project, something that could be completed within a short time frame.

After meeting with John and delivering all of the necessary information, I didn't hear from him for several months. Being one of those individuals who appreciates customer service, I started to question John's methods of follow-through. I must confess I had a few preconceived notions about professionals, particularly those professionals who had earned licenses. I believed (and still do) that a license comes with a higher expectation of service, which includes promptly returned phone calls and e-mails.

Because John had not returned my phone calls or e-mails, I started to grow anxious. To complicate matters, I was leaving on a long trip overseas and my time was at a premium.

My level of enthusiasm for John's professional services had taken a definite plunge. In the following chapters, the reasons why customers lose faith in businesses will be discussed further. This is one of the worst outcomes within a customer service system, and any attempts to restore confidence will become strained.

Two days before I was scheduled to leave, John's secretary (his very faithful and dedicated secretary) called to ask if I had time to travel to John's office to sign documents. This seemed like a positive turn of events. I informed her about my impending trip and time constraints. I was sure John already knew this because I had communicated my circumstances during all of those earlier phone messages and e-mails.

John's secretary called again, and this time she was even more apologetic. Under the circumstances, I wasn't very receptive. However, what she said next did get my attention. She asked me if it would be appropriate for John to make a personal visit to my home; he wanted to deliver the papers in person.

Of course, I agreed, and even after I had hung up the phone, I couldn't help but feel impressed. My million-dollar-an-hour attorney (I'm exaggerating here) was going to set aside his busy workday and visit me at home bearing the documents that needed my signature. I realized that based on both the type of transaction and the time constraints, a courier service would have been out of the question, and the only other option was to send an office representative or notary.

The absurdity of this situation didn't end there. John sat in traffic for two hours on the way to my house. We signed the documents and were together for a total of thirty minutes before he left. He didn't even have a cup of coffee.

During those thirty minutes, John explained his reasons for the delays. His father had died earlier that summer, then he had been very ill for several months. His expertise required specific legal information, and he had been too ill to provide both.

I must admit, my initial reaction was unkind. I didn't feel sympathetic to John's personal circumstances or his illness. From a business perspective, poor customer service jeopardizes professional standing and future business performance. In addition, when service is compromised, the business entity has a duty to offer alternative options to prevent the loss of valuable customers and company brand reputation. For example, I have never seen a McDonald's restaurant remain closed when the restaurant manager was too ill to open the doors. High-quality service is thus a continuous process that does not tolerate interruptions.

Perhaps also relevant, his particular legal transaction could not have been a priority to John or his firm. However, John had gone out of his way to restore service satisfaction. The solutions had a subliminal outcome; they allowed me to "feel" like a valuable customer and reinforced my loyalty. Most significant, John had been willing to take responsibility and resolve a situation of his own creation.

It struck me that if global customer service could emulate this standard, under many unstable business conditions, competition could be neutralized and thereby produce a greater number of profitable outcomes.

The goal of this book is to improve all customer interactions by establishing a service system that supports the entire organization or business.

Since every facet of revenue generation involves customer participation, distinguishing whether the customer is internal or external bares little significance to the overall service delivery practice, which must always remain high.

Mastering the first step of this new, emboldened service system requires customer identification by "type."This process incorporates the concepts in this book, which are relatively straightforward. After implementation, the organization's mission, purpose and profitability become positively enriched by both future brand placement (if one exists) and a reduced level of customer migration to the competition.

Customer Identification contributes to the positive flow of all business systems and most important, the continued satisfaction of all contributing customers.

~ ~ ~

During highly effective communication, all three Service Monkeys—See, Say, and Do—are fully represented.

The See Monkey introduces a win-win approach that supports positive interactions between the service delivery organization and the customer.

The See Monkey offers strategies that potentially diffuse service dissatisfaction by promoting loyalty and elevating the significance of the company brand.

The primary objective of the See Monkey is to manage customer retention.

Chapter One

Fairy-Tale Manufacturing

"I don't know what your destiny will be, but one thing I know: the ones among you who will be really happy are those who have sought and found how to serve."

—Albert Schweitzer

Made in America?

Why does anyone buy anything foreign made? Buying American seems to make sense; after all, we live in America, don't we?

Why buy products made in China, India, or elsewhere? Wouldn't it be more practical, not to mention patriotic, to buy products stamped with that all-important label that proudly states "Made in America"?

As history suggests, American ingenuity has received an outpouring of positive global attention over the decades. This popularity began in the nineteenth century during the Industrial Revolution. However, it was not until after the Second World War that the manufacturing sector began a significant expansion. This expansion produced a burgeoning middle class that now had more money to spend on goods and services.

During a long period of economic expansion that spanned over sixty years, there were many significant advancements and innovations. Commodities such as steel, wireless communication, and the Internet have produced a greater demand for goods manufactured in all parts of the world. All of these innovations have altered life as we know it and influenced everything from how we travel to how we do business.

As part of this new and expanding global economy, the industrial sectors worldwide have contributed to the overall growth of business. In the new millennium, the most influential of these sectors is the one commonly referred to as "service."

Monkey Dynamics

The Service Monkeys, who will be formerly introduced in the next chapter, believe that there is a strong relationship between the manufacturing health of a country and the robust state of its employment. In the United States, a diminishing manufacturing sector and the reduction of new manufacturing orders have produced an unexpected redistribution of the workforce to other industry sectors (see Figure 1-1).

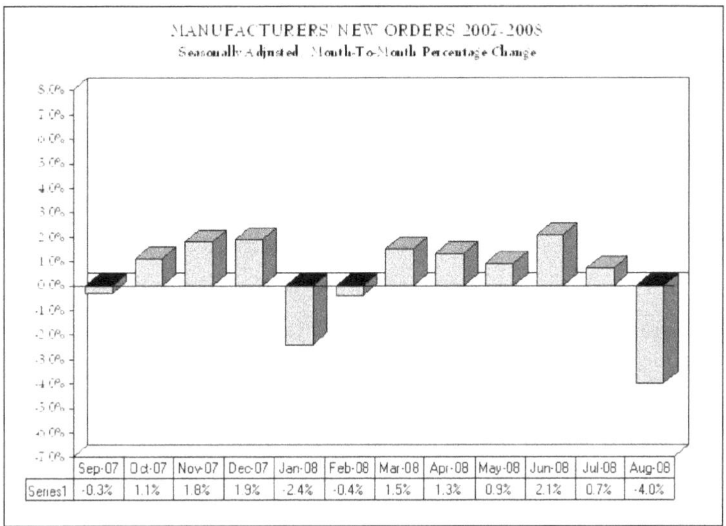

Figure 1-1. Decline of New Orders – Manufacturing. Source: U.S. Census Bureau.

Monkey Employment

Because of higher earnings and a flexible taxation system, American consumers have considerable buying influence. A large and employed workforce spends more post-taxed dollars, and this in turn stimulates greater worldwide economic buoyancy.

When compared to other nations of similar size and economic significance, the United States may be one of the few countries in the world where the unemployment rate per capita is small compared to the cumulative earning population. Between July 1998 and July 2008, the unemployment figures for the U.S. ranged between 4.5 percent and 5.7 percent (see figure 1-2). These are relatively low in relation to the total number of people who are employed.

However, a shrinking manufacturing sector and the rearrangement of jobs within all industry sectors have produced an unexpected outcome: an expansion of the service industry. This unplanned job migration has only served to displace skills and produce lower-grade positions and fewer growth opportunities.

Over the last decade, education requirements for American workers have also advanced; however, salary growth has stagnated. When considering customary job trends, improved wage conditions are often dependent upon improving employee skills, which relies on adding training and increasing the number of apprenticeships. These provisions may be viewed as common within manufacturing; however, they are not as prevalent within the service sector. The overall outcome has been more jobs, fewer skills, and less training.

Year	Jan	Feb	Mar	Apr	May	Jun	Jul	Aug	Sep	Oct	Nov	Dec
2000	4.0	4.1	4.0	3.8	4.0	4.0	4.0	4.1	3.9	3.9	3.9	3.9
2001	4.2	4.2	4.3	4.4	4.3	4.5	4.6	4.9	5.0	5.3	5.5	5.7
2002	5.7	5.7	5.7	5.9	5.8	5.8	5.8	5.7	5.7	5.7	5.9	6.0
2003	5.8	5.9	5.9	6.0	6.1	6.3	6.2	6.1	6.1	6.0	5.8	5.7
2004	5.7	5.6	5.8	5.6	5.6	5.6	5.5	5.4	5.4	5.5	5.4	5.4
2005	5.2	5.4	5.2	5.1	5.1	5.0	5.0	4.9	5.1	5.0	5.0	4.8
2006	4.7	4.7	4.7	4.7	4.7	4.6	4.7	4.7	4.5	4.4	4.5	4.4
2007	4.6	4.5	4.4	4.5	4.5	4.6	4.7	4.7	4.7	4.8	4.7	5.0
2008	4.9	4.8	5.1	5.0	5.5	5.5	5.7	6.1	6.1			

Figure 1-2. Unemployment Population Survey. Source: Bureau of Labor Statistics.

Buying Influence

A growing demand for cheaper high-quality goods has also produced a reliance on imports (see figure 1-3), particularly when products are no longer manufactured in the United States.

The Service Monkeys refer to this rapid increase of product imports as exceptional buying influence, or EBI.

EBI can also be described as a shift in buying trends from developed nations to developing nations, like China and India, who have methodically increased their manufacturing output.

Technology innovation has also accelerated EBI in these developing nations. This has resulted in an unprecedented expansion of manufacturing in less than a decade, which over the course of history is a relatively short period of rapid growth when compared to similar surges in manufacturing.

Another indirect influence of EBI has been an abundant and available surplus of "modern" raw materials. Historically, during previous manufacturing expansion periods, these products were more expensive to produce or simply not available. This list of raw materials has expanded to include newer innovations such as plastic and fiber optics, which have improved communication channels among industry sectors.

Greater access to these raw materials has accelerated manufacturing output and also produced an unfavorable and progressive condition: increased competition.

Fueling competition, developing countries like China and India have been less concerned with product performance, customer service, and quality, and more focused on meeting supply demands.

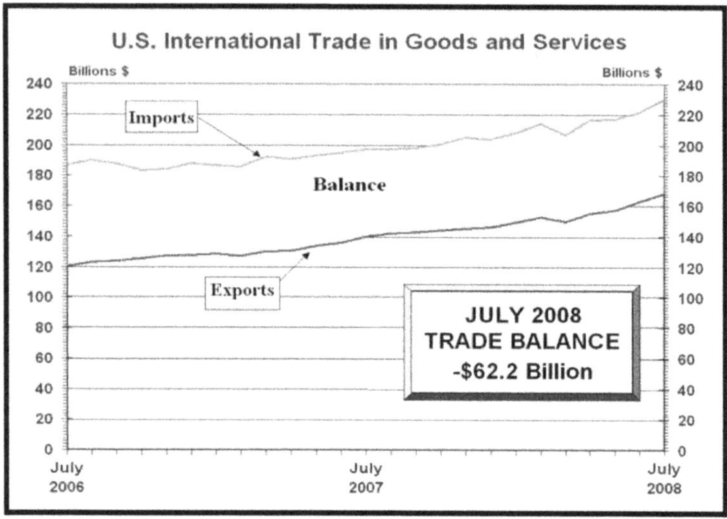

Figure 1-3. U.S. International Trade in Goods and Services. Source: U.S. Census Bureau.

Monkey Chapter Overview

- Buying American-made products is not only patriotic but critical to establishing superior global economic influence.
- A gradual decline of manufacturing in developed nations has produced a migration of jobs to other industrial sectors, which in turn has expanded the role of service.
- The expansion of the service sector is attributed to the growing demand for goods and services and a rise in consumer spending.
- The service sector is most susceptible to job loss during times of recession.

- EBI represents a shift in increased buying influence from developed nations to developing nations who have increased their manufacturing output.

~ ~ ~

Chapter Two

Service-Bound Monkey

"We must become the change we want to see."
—Mahatma Gandhi

Meet the Service Monkeys

The three Service Monkeys are symbolic. They represent creative expression, which improves existing, repetitive, and often unproductive business behaviors.

Certain monkeys, and specifically great apes such as chimpanzees, share 98.76 percent gene similarity with humans in their DNA. In captivity, chimpanzees communicate by mimicking, repeating, and imitating, as seen by their ability to use American Sign Language for comprehension.[1] These multifaceted behaviors allow chimps to learn and adapt to their environment.

Exemplary customer service, or Monkey Service, relies on creative, non-repetitive behaviors. Monkey systems are unique because they focus on open access and never rely on pure technology to manage service outcomes.

Within organizations, the established employee culture is the mechanism that delivers these high-quality service practices. The employee culture is viewed as the foundation for the Monkey service system, and the driving force for all successful business outcomes. To ignore the relevance of the employee culture is akin to ignoring the purpose and progressive direction of the entire organization.

Monkey Objective

The goal of the Monkey service system is to resolve customer inquiries to completion, regardless of where these inquiries originated.

The three advantages of using a solution-based system include identifying and catering to specific customer types, maintaining customer retention, and managing the placement of the company's brand in the product marketplace.

Monkey Service recognizes customer retention as the highest priority of any organization because customers represent the cost of marketing, business reputation, and future profits. Customer retention is the single most important variable because it influences all business decisions.

Monkey Behaviors

In the wild, monkeys live in family groups. Their roles within these families necessitate that they render certain services, which are reinforced through a series of routine behaviors. These services include grooming, feeding, and nurturing. Compared to humans, wild monkeys have a primitive form of awareness, and this is what limits the types of services they can provide.

Chimpanzees deliver these services to other chimpanzees, but not to other species of great apes or other animals. Grooming, feeding, and nurturing are considered non-creative and instinctual, and are necessary to ensure the survival of the species.

In contrast, business survival is not primitive but complex. Business survival utilizes multiple systems, which perform as they are designed. When considering the whole system, its responsibilities include managing market share, enforcing uniform hiring practices, elevating brand recognition, and regulating all quality and performance standards.

The most significant issue impacting all service systems is the amount of revenue spent in relation to the number of customers the organization can retain. Customer retention must therefore adjust to changing conditions, the most important of these conditions being customer satisfaction and the role of competition.

Elevating Performance

Chimpanzees are known to be competent learners. The service solution system relies on employee training as the primary business tool that is used to improve company performance standards.

The most significant advantage of training is the ability to direct the employee culture. When service agents are trained, the opportunities to effect greater revenue performance become a feature of open access. Training allows service agents to use predetermined tools and solutions to elevate customer satisfaction standards, promote the company's brand, and build loyalty by regulating customer retention.

Monkey Chapter Overview

- The Service Monkeys represent a shift in business focus from the repetitive to the creative. They resolve customer issues by offering customized service solutions that elevate customer satisfaction.
- Within any organization, there may be multiple service systems. When combined, the objective of the greater service system is to improve customer retention and maintain consistent revenue performance.
- Within Monkey solution systems, every trained employee is capable of delivering a higher standard of customer service.
- Customer retention is the single most influential business variable.
- The goal of the Monkey service system is to resolve customer inquiries to completion, regardless of where these inquiries originated.

~ ~ ~

The Monkey Service Hourglass

Chapter Three

Customer Types

Gerard's Proverb

A westerner met an African while traveling. He asked how far and how long it would take to arrive at a destination. Not waiting for a response the westerner proceeded to take out his maps and compass, and began making complex distance measurements. During this process he noticed that the African was smiling at him.

He asked: "Do you already know how long the journey will take?"

The African replied: "My friend, the journey will take as long as it will. The time taken depends on who you meet along the way and what you are willing to do to get to your destination."

—*Unknown author*

Customer Service Hourglass

Whenever customers initiate communication with a company, they automatically enter what the Service Monkeys describe as the "hourglass." After entering the hourglass (usually after the purchase of a product or service), a customer's loyalty to the company will depend upon the level of service provided by the organization.

The service hourglass is used to identify the buying behaviors of specific Monkey customer types, and to monitor customer retention during various business cycles.

Expensive Customers

Within Monkey solution systems, customer retention relies on the combined expenses of advertising and marketing. This is the cost associated with special promotions and other incentives used to deliver and retain each customer type in the service hourglass at any time. There are three established Monkey customer types: Constants, Hunters, and Untouchables.

Monkey Type 1: The Constant

This customer type pays his or her bills on time and, in the Monkeys' opinion, is the best customer to collect in the service hourglass.

Constants are identified by brand loyalty. They remain loyal regardless of buying trends or economic shifts. They always make purchase decisions based on both quality and brand, rather than by value or incentive.

These customers are to be appreciated above all other customer types because they prefer the status quo, and are not adventurous when it comes to seeking out product incentives or promotions. They represent the mid-quantity of customers in the service hourglass and are typically repeat buyers. They remain loyal to the brand, except when the brand diminishes in quality.

Unfortunately, because of growing competition, Constants are slowly becoming a "dying breed."

Constant Identifiers:
1) Quality; 2) Brand; 3) Service Delivery.

Monkey Type 2: The Hunter

Hunters are the exact opposite of Constants.

The number of Hunters in the service hourglass will increase over time because of competition.

The Hunter's goal is to purchase goods and services based specifically on price. The Hunter has little or no brand loyalty. Hunters determine their own standards for what they consider fair business practices. They will quibble about almost anything, including company procedures. The number of Hunters in comparison to Constants in the service hourglass is always greater.

Hunters never value brand, which makes them the most unpredictable customer type. They also tend to stay in the service hourglass for the shortest period of time, moving to the competition if better incentives are offered. The more discounts and promotions available in the marketplace, the more likely Hunters will abandon both the company and the brand.

A business is more apt to exchange Hunters for more Hunters within the service hourglass, particularly when the business offers regular incentives and promotions.

Because the nature of the Hunter is unpredictable, the cost of doing business with this customer type is often the greatest portion of marketing and advertising expense.

Solving Hunter service inquiries with fluidity and urgency becomes critical to managing customer retention, market share and revenue growth. The largest marketing expense is devoted to attracting and retaining Hunters in the service hourglass.

When a company loses Hunters, this represents a lack of understanding of customer retention. These conditions arise because of a combination of service practices that are unable to adapt to a changing customer type environment. These conditions include inexperienced service agents and the use of poorly planned technology.

Because the Hunter is the most frequent user of customer service, the goal of the solution system is to manage and retain Hunters well beyond the point that they originally demand service.

Retaining Hunters is dependent upon the difference between the cost of adding superior employee training versus the ever-increasing cost of marketing.

Hunter Identifiers:
1) Price; 2) Increased Service; 3) Convenience of Use.

Monkey Type 3: The Untouchable

Untouchables are unlikely to require service on a regular basis. They have neither the time nor the understanding to care for trivial issues that may arise in the course of common business transactions.

The Untouchables usually employs Constants and Hunters to act on their behalf to resolve their service issues. Untouchables never identify with brand and consequently have no brand loyalty.

When an Untouchable is forced to seek out customer service, he or she has a specific issue that needs immediate resolution.

A high level of service quality is required to resolve Untouchable inquiries because Untouchables demand more direct attention. If dissatisfied with service quality, Untouchables tend to cause the most damage to a company's brand because of their ability to influence other customer types.

Untouchables represent the smallest number of customers in the service hourglass; however, they are the most influential when it comes to their ability to direct the course of the company's brand and reputation.

Untouchable Identifiers:
1) Superior Service; 2) Immediate Resolution.

Monkey Bridge

Are there overlapping customer types?

In the wild, a great ape can be classified as a chimpanzee or an orangutan, but it can never be classified as a lion. The Service Monkeys believe that there is very little overlap among customer types.

The definitions of customer types are based more on emotional buying patterns, which rarely change even during periods of economic prosperity when consumers have more money to spend.

By asking a series of customized questions, the buying patterns of most customers can be identified, which allows service agents to offer more precise solutions when they are resolving customer inquiries.

Identifying Customer Types

The questions asked identify both the customer type being served and the level of service required to complete the customer's inquiry. For example, when a customer requests a change in his or her general account profile such as address or other personal account information, this is typically a Constant inquiry. Note, because these services are generally automated, Constants may require more time to adapt to new technology. To ensure greater retention of Constants, less technology complexity and more direct service options offer ease of use to the overall solution system.

Constants tend to pay on time and as a general rule do not incur service or late fees. When Constants find unusual or unexpected charges on their bills, they may or may not become upset, but they do expect immediate resolution. Their loyalty to the brand is reflected in their acceptance of the solutions being offered.

It is vital that Constants are handled with the utmost respect and given a great deal of attention because they represent the greatest level of brand loyalty in the service hourglass. Their numbers, although small, are significant to managing customer retention.

Most important, Constants require the least amount of marketing expense to retain, and they are always repeat buyers.

~ ~ ~

In contrast, Hunter inquiries are many and varied. They range in topic from price and expense to quality issues and inaccurate billing. Hunters may also have inquiries that require a higher level of expertise, investigation, and follow-up to resolve.

Of all the three customer types, the Hunter will require the greatest amount of immediate and customized service.

Hunters are valuable because they represent the largest portion of a company's revenue loss, gain, and marketing expense.

The Service Monkeys wish to point out that the number of Hunters entering the service hourglass will always fluctuate. The service agent's goal is to lengthen the Hunter's stay in the hourglass and thereby reduce marketing expense.

~ ~ ~

Untouchables ask direct, specific questions. They are astute and generally unwilling to compromise.

Untouchables will call customer service because they have been placed in a situation where they must personally resolve a service issue. As far as this customer type is concerned, the circumstances warrant their intervention.

Untouchables will offer less information and represent the most difficult customer type to communicate with because they perceive the situation as a waste of their time. Untouchables are likely to lose their tempers easily and will show extreme impatience.

Untouchable issues must be handled with urgency and the highest level of customer care. Service agents are encouraged to be vigilant when dealing with Untouchables because this customer type can destroy brand recognition with very little effort. Their power to influence is what makes them the most unique of all three customer types.

Monkey Chapter Overview

- The service hourglass is the most valuable Monkey customer retention tool. It is used to determine the overall cost of customer service based on the marketing and advertising expense required to retain each of the three Monkey customer types.
- There are three predominant Monkey customer types: Constants, Hunters, and Untouchables.
- The service hourglass can be an effective tool for managing customer retention throughout the entire organization because it monitors the number of customers retained during business cycles.
- A convenient method of monitoring customer types requires tracking the number of promotional incentives that each customer takes advantage of.
- Customer types can be identified by using a series of specific and customized questions.

- Identifying customer types is the first step toward offering precise solutions and resolving customer service inquiries to completion.

~ ~ ~

Chapter Four

Trained to Push Buttons

"A well-informed mind is the best security against the contagion of folly and of vice. The vacant mind is ever on the watch for relief, and ready to plunge into error, to escape from the languor of idleness."

—Ann Radcliffe, The Mysteries of Udolpho, 1764

New Customer Evolution

In the new millennium, technology is so widely used that it has displaced workers and streamlined product delivery systems so that they are no longer creative or user-friendly.

How customers adapt to these technology-driven environments influences how companies deliver service. The risk exists that customers will be unwilling to adapt to technology, and in these situations, the influence of the customer extends to how he or she picks and chooses the vendors that he or she will do business with.

Monkey Competition

Poorly planned technology produces greater customer dissatisfaction. For example, dissatisfied with service quality, Hunters are more apt to seek out competitive vendors who have similar products but may or may not provide better services.

Companies that insist on relying on technology rather than investing in employee training are subject to a diminished awareness of customer retention requirements. Under these conditions, both customer retention and brand integrity suffer.

Service Stability

Successful inquiry resolution depends on the quantity of inquiries that need to be resolved, how many customized service options are available, and the time required to resolve each issue to completion.

The more the customer is included in the resolution process, the more likely the customer will remain loyal to the company brand and stay in the service hourglass.

Solution Customer Service

When solution customer service is practiced throughout the organization, the overall quality of service improves, and this in turn produces a higher level of customer satisfaction.

Employee Training: The Three Keys

- Employee training generates timely resolution of even the most difficult customer inquiries.
- Employee training adapts solutions to the inquiry volume and the complexity of service issues.
- Employee training ensures that the greatest majority of service inquiries can be resolved at the first customer interaction, which promotes improved brand recognition.

Why Provide Employee Training?

Within solution systems, training is a regulatory device that manages business growth and stability over time. When used in conjunction with everyday business processes, employee training improves the overall company reputation and extends the life of the company's brand.

Employee training produces a more vibrant company culture. Trained employees are more likely to participate at a higher level and utilize their company skills to offer customers varied inquiry solutions that elevate brand integrity.

High-Quality Solution Training = A Managed Employee Culture

Solution Utility

The solution utility represents the training model utilized by the entire organization.

The solution utility manages the flow of the service system. The utility also monitors the effectiveness of employee training and identifies any necessary training adjustments.

During periods of erratic sales volume (up or down) and unexpected economic shifts that impact the general product marketplace, the solution utility continues to manage customers by maintaining a higher standard of service delivery.

The utility combines employee training with customized solutions. This combination of resources can control the most unmanageable of customer inquiries by delivering the appropriate solutions.

Establishing a utility system also maintains a synergy between the solutions offered and the technology tools that are part of the service system, which will include phone trees and voice mail.

Solution Utility = The Organization's Overall Training System

Training Levels: Review

The scope and complexity of customer issues determines the number of trained service agents that will be needed to support the solution service system.

The level of service agent training will be determined by the quantity of service inquiries and the numbers of each customer type that the service system has been designed to support.

Monkey Chapter Overview

- The solution utility is described as the organization-wide service training system.
- The training system operates to unify the entire organization.
- The solution utility establishes the foundation for a participating employee culture that indirectly maintains customer retention.

~ ~ ~

Chapter Five

Beware of the Competition

Webster's definition of evolve:
"develop, unfold, open out; produce."

Advancing Civilizations

During the last decade, developing nations such as China and India have been able to increase manufacturing output and meet the demands for cheaper high-quality goods worldwide.

By enforcing strategic currency control measures, these countries have been able to create economic conditions that have stimulated rapid industrial growth. In fact, over a mere five-to-seven-year period these countries have undergone accelerated economic expansion, which has resulted in the fastest manufacturing surge ever experienced in human history. This growth can be compared to a mini yet mighty industrial revolution.

This spurt in industrial activity has been bolstered by technology sharing, a very unique condition, particularly when no country in the past has had such access to technology during a period of manufacturing explosion.

Another tremendous advantage has been access to raw materials, which are now widely available and cheaper to produce. This access has contributed to fewer delays in the overall manufacturing process.

The infrastructure of China and India could also be considered primed for growth. Both of these countries have a large and relatively cheap labor force, which is paid below the average earnings of developed nations.

In combination with having political and taxation systems that have fewer regulations, these developing nations have wholeheartedly embraced manufacturing, not only as a means to reduce national unemployment but also to reduce global debt and improve infrastructure expansion. With so many favorable conditions, increasing manufacturing output has realized a significant source of untold economic wealth.

No Longer Made in America

Overseas manufacturing has met the American consumer demand for a wide variety of cheaper goods from milk products to advanced computer technology. The Service Monkeys describe the growing dependency on overseas manufacturing as a "reverse economy." This condition has produced a shift in economic supremacy in favor of developing nations who now control the world product supply.

This new dynamic has not only encouraged a greater demand for cheaper goods and more competition, but has also created unrealistic earnings expectations of companies in developed nations who no longer manufacture or control the costs of their own product lines.

A Competitive Advantage

The erosion of domestic manufacturing in the United States has required importing goods from developing countries who can manufacture them at a lower cost.

In the United States, the importing of goods and the outsourcing of services have produced a redistribution of expertise and placed emphasis on a highly educated but unskilled workforce. However, while education and the rate of product sophistication has improved, more service experience plus skills and training have become necessary to support the vast array of products that now flood the marketplace.

Surplus Conditions

The variety and quantity of goods that are manufactured in developing countries have created a global surplus condition. Controlling this surplus has necessitated more product support and created more jobs in the service sector.

Having so many products has caused the service environment to be inundated with customer inquiries. The most unsatisfactory outcome has been the inability to properly manage these inquiries using technologies that cannot be expanded easily or customized.

Unfortunately, within these Western developed markets, this surplus also represents uncontrollable competition and the need for organizations to offer a higher standard of customer support. The Service Monkeys describe this condition as EBI, or exceptional buying influence, the concept introduced in chapter one.

EBI is a condition that accelerates during times when there is excessive competition and fluctuating customer retention.

A Single-Focus Response

Monitoring customer retention relies on service systems that are equipped to manage inquiry resolutions and revenue performance, while at the same time elevate brand reputation.

The service systems that exist today are inadequate because they are heavily driven by technology and are better described as static. These systems represent a duplication of effort and expense, and in general lack the ingenuity that can offer customers superior service options.

In addition, when there are so many products flooding the consumer marketplace, service requires specialization and product knowledge. An example of this is the influx of cell phones and computers. Although these products may have been manufactured using similar technologies, often there are multiple brands and different features that require more service options.

As more products enter the global marketplace, static service templates will be unable to adapt to the quantity and variety of customer inquiries.

Monkey Disadvantage

Although India and China have been able to deliver large volumes of products to Western consumer markets, Western markets have been unable to manage the service delivery process. Recent examples include the 2007 lead paint scares, which impacted American toy manufacturers and resulted in dramatic product recalls.[2]

Another, more serious situation involved food imports and the outbreak of a lethal food-borne illness, which sickened consumers and resulted in the deaths of people and animals who ate the tainted foods.[3]

In September 2008, a British chocolate maker reported findings that indicated traces of the drug melamine in chocolates produced at one of the company's factories in Beijing.[4] Although this had not produced any fatal outcomes, the company responded by recalling eleven types of its chocolate. A previous milk scandal, which had erupted earlier that month, identified that melamine had been found in milk powder and was linked to kidney stones in children.

Even in situations where overseas factories use template instructions, the monitoring process is often compromised by cultural roadblocks, which result in remote and inferior quality standards that have far-reaching and often dangerous consequences.

Monkey Training

As manufacturing outsourcing becomes more popular, the need to manage these unusual conditions becomes the responsibility of trained employees in the country of product distribution.

Effective employee training can improve the service delivery that produces customized solutions to service inquiries.

When employees are untrained, a company environment is created that is disconnected with the needs of its customers, and this indirectly increases the threat of competition.

Brand Saturation

There are many brands and varieties of cell phones, but usually only one level of expertise is available to resolve the technical issues of all.

In many organizations, the first service level is basic and regulated by technology-driven templates. It is interesting that this service level receives the greatest number of customer inquiries and is supported by agents who have the least amount of training.

Automated systems lose effectiveness because they are not continuously monitored or updated to offer new service solutions. The severity of the situation becomes compounded when service agents are unable to deliver expanded service options because the technology they use is limited.

The next level of service is equally deficient and is described as the technical support level. In most situations, technicians can respond to technology issues but have limited knowledge when it comes to expanding company brand recognition and managing customer retention.

Monkey Chapter Overview

- Over the last decade, the number of jobs in the customer service sector has increased while the number of manufacturing sector jobs has declined.
- Often redundant and expensive technologies manage the entire business environment, which includes the service delivery system.
- An overuse of technology has produced a reliance on static service templates, which has produced poor-quality service and encouraged customers to migrate to the competition.
- Trained service agents improve customer retention by encouraging a higher level of customer interaction.
- When customers are given more service options, more positive attention is directed to the company's brand.
- Solution customer service manages customer retention and creates opportunities for companies to increase revenue by delivering more precise services and products.

~ ~ ~

Chapter Six

Monkey Migration

Webster's definition of serve:
"work under another; carry out duties; treat in a specific way."

Consequences of Global Expansion

Although growing in volume and capacity, employee wages and education requirements within the service sector have contracted, forcing an overly educated workforce to move into underpaid positions. The relationship between qualifications and modified salary may not be so unique for a sector that does not require any specific skills or advanced technical training. This dynamic has also produced less job mobility, not only within organizations but throughout the sector.

The main cause of reduced job mobility has been the elimination of in-house job training. This condition has encouraged a reliance on redundant technologies, which has not only replaced jobs, but also encouraged the creation of a disposable, unskilled, and migratory workforce.

Service Quality

The expansion of the service sector has also created a new and unusual hiring condition: the demand for an educated versus skilled worker.

Imposing educational requirements supports a greater payroll expense. The organizational response to increased payroll expenses has been to replace the number of required service employees with technology-driven templates and overseas outsourcing. These two unregulated variables have produced a service environment that operates with fewer workers who have fewer skills.

Finally, outsourcing has not only caused the loss of American jobs, but also created a duplication in service expenses.

Tech Stuff

A heavy reliance on support technologies such as phone trees, databases, and other automated services has diminished service quality.

As service standards continue to deteriorate, customers will experience greater frustration, particularly when it comes to operating technologies that have been designed as "self-help" service systems.

Waiting on hold for long periods and being transferred across phone tree systems have produced unnecessary interruptions in the service delivery process. Unfortunately, these negative associations extend long after the initial service interaction and are detrimental to managing long-term customer retention.

Futuristic Service

Monkey service systems support a more customized approach to service delivery, which promotes open communication between customers and the organization. Increasing human contact within service delivery elevates the importance of the company brand and strengthens the employee culture.

Monkey Quality

Because the global economy cannot be controlled, there will always be a large variety of goods available, and these goods will always cost more to produce.

As technology improves, greater consumer expectations will promote the growth of competition. New products will continue to flood the general marketplace, and this will cause service inquiries to increase in volume and complexity.

Because the majority of customer inquiries are post-sales, these inquiries will cause fluctuations in revenue. Service systems that are dependent upon technology will be unable to adjust to these variable conditions and will have to be replaced.

Finding it difficult to adapt to technology or improve employee training, several companies have attempted to charge fees for technical support. The Service Monkeys cannot imagine what value this offers to the company, the company's brand, or the long-range impact on customer retention.

Certain products, when a warranty is not offered, may require fee-based services. However, these fees should be secondary to a variety of no-charge service options that address complex issues and are available to customers under all service conditions.

Monkey Changes

Fluctuating inquiry volumes will determine the rate of increased outsourcing and the continued expansion of the service sector, particularly in developed nations.

The combined effect of the decline in manufacturing influence and the rise of technology use has already produced what could be termed as an "economic quickening" condition that continues to threaten industry-wide employment. To offer direct examples, consider how ATMs have replaced positions once held by bank tellers, and how online shopping has impacted retail store clerks. Automation has also replaced attendants at service stations, and many of the larger grocery chains have installed self-checkout areas.

These trends are on the rise, and although they appear to make life more efficient for consumers, they have also created a reduction in direct customer service and eliminated many traditional occupations.

It would be remiss to omit the obvious here; entities that sell products or services but refuse to invest in high-quality customer service systems will suffer the most.

Customer Influence

As technology use increases, there has been a reduction of service access and, more important, a reduction in interpersonal service interactions. By limiting access, companies have prompted customers, who have nowhere else to go to resolve their own inquiries, and to question whether they made the right decision by purchasing these particular products and services.

In situations where customers do initiate dialogue, these interactions represent the initial point of contact at which the purchaser activates the terms of the original sale or warranty.

The relationship to the original purchase has little to do with the salesperson who sold the product, but more so with the information that was provided about the warranty when the product was sold.

This initial contact is considered a critical stage in the service delivery cycle because both the organization and the customer are now focused on their own interpretations of the original terms of the sale.

At this point, the customer has been placed in a position where he or she can evaluate how the company performs, not only in relation to the product purchased, but also to the implied warranties or service commitments that came with the product. This interaction represents a validation of certain promises made at the time of the purchase and is construed as a test of strength of the company's commitment to its products and the quality of its employee training.

The Branding Iron

The Service Monkeys consider brand to be the overall compliment to product performance—brand being the ultimate measurement of a company's stability.

Company stability is the relationship between the service response and how willing the company is to make things right when things go wrong. Because product performance and marketplace endurance cannot be guaranteed, the quality of service becomes the most reliable indicator of brand strength over time.

Service Quality = Brand Recognition

Employee Service Expense

The combined influence of high-quality service and brand integrity maintains company longevity, particularly during volatile economic conditions such as a recession or times when there are lags in product research and development.

As the global economy expands, the propensity for recession trends will become more frequent. The "quickening" condition described earlier will accelerate, particularly as technology becomes more sophisticated and as worldwide manufacturing is taken over by developing nations.

A New Service Era

Having a strong service organization reduces the reliance on outsourcing. Investing in manpower and training employees helps to minimize the impact of poor management decisions and any deficits in quality control.

Introducing high-quality employee training also increases knowledge about products and operational systems. Having greater product knowledge produces efficient and conclusive responses to customer inquiries. For example, having five or six computer brands, not to mention several hundred computer options, may require specific service expertise. Training offers this expertise and eliminates redundant hiring practices and overstaffing.

The Technology Challenge

Having fewer workers and redundant automation results in increased costs in technology, technology support, education for technology, and the added cost associated with upgrading technology systems. These costs become magnified by the time and expense required to first adapt the business infrastructure to support these new systems, and then to monitor overseas outsourcing systems, particularly when there may be cultural barriers to overcome.

As the consumer market demands more goods, the use of non-adaptive technologies will increase and encourage a growing reliance on inefficient tools like impersonal form letters and e-mail. These tools are considered inefficient because they fail to manage customer retention.

Another unforeseen impact of technology has been the de-focusing of company brand. Poor technology planning has contributed to negative customer reactions and poor service inquiry management. When there is a lack of employee training, technology cannot be relied upon to improve service delivery, particularly in situations where service has been outsourced to a foreign country.

Monkey Chapter Overview

- Both customer retention and customer loyalty are valuable measurements of service delivery standards within the entire organization.
- Having frustrated and angry customers has far-reaching consequences, particularly when attempting to manage customer retention.
- The increasing use of form letters, e-mail, and phone trees, though they are simplifications, has deteriorated service quality, destroyed customer loyalty, and diminished customer retention.
- Using unmonitored technologies in combination with fewer trained employees impacts overall company productivity.
- Investing in redundant technologies not only creates a greater long-term expense, but also replaces the human creative capacity that delivers "outside the box" customer service solutions.

~ ~ ~

Chapter Seven

Continuous Civility

Webster's definition of customer:
"one who enters a shop to buy, esp. one who deals regularly with it."

Continuous Civility

Positioning the company's brand becomes vital to managing customer retention and resolving customer service inquiries in an efficient manner. Understanding the value of brand requires the company to evaluate customer needs and to improve communication.

Within the Monkey service system, the relationship between brand and customer loyalty is described as "continuous civility."

Continuous civility produces a higher standard of business performance regardless of economic conditions, poor management decisions, or lulls in product research and development. Continuous civility is also the mechanism that influences future customer purchase decisions.

Continuous civility affects all consumer markets, even those products that are overly technical and time sensitive. Trained service agents deliver continuous civility using solution tools.

Gone Missing

Not every service interaction will result in a fully resolved customer inquiry. Poor service interactions will result in customer dissatisfaction, which will negatively impact customer retention. Customers and revenue that "go missing" are representative of a service system that offers limited customer solutions.

Customer losses can be minimized when service delivery systems identify and regulate customer types.

Creating the Connection

Perhaps the most recognizable shift in customer loyalty happens when a customer takes advantage of the competition. These conditions occur more frequently when technology improves and many varieties of the same product enter the marketplace, which creates a competitive atmosphere.

For example, the Hunter customer type does not value loyalty when making purchase decisions. For Hunters, the lure of the sale is not necessarily the product or the services offered, but the additional value that is being delivered before, during, and after making the purchase.

To reduce the number of customers that go missing, continuous civility demands a higher quality of service in order to create a stronger connection between the customer and the company's brand.

The Outcome

Why allow customers to leave?

The Service Monkeys believe that this is often unintentional and due to a lack of understanding of how to manage the various customer types. This seems to contradict the expense, time, and attention expended by marketing and advertising organizations to attract customers to buy products and services.

If the organization remains unaware of how to manage customer retention, the service delivery system will continue to produce poor service outcomes and fewer customers retained.

The good news is, these conditions can be identified and monitored. The service system can be designed so that it delivers specific and customized questions that first identify customer types and then resolve service inquiries to completion.

Continuous Civility Practice

The following sample questions assist in creating the foundation for a continuous civility practice. The answers to these questions can help to identify what happens when customers do "go missing."

- When did this customer buy the initial product or service?
- Did this purchase require a promotion to initiate the sale?

- Which customer type left the service hourglass; was it a Constant, Hunter, or Untouchable?
- Why did these customers stop buying products or services? List multiple reasons (if any).
- What incentives did the competition offer to interest these customers?
- What could the company have done differently to ensure that these customers stayed?
- After these customers left, what was done to encourage them to return?

Activating Service

How much advertising and marketing expense is spent to convince new and returning customers to call a toll-free number to purchase products and services, or simply to make a service inquiry?

Making the call is often the easy part; what happens next makes all the difference between customers lost and customers gained.

Managing the first customer interaction is critical to establishing a series of unspoken service variables. The most important of these variables is customer loyalty.

Another description for these variables is the implied warranty, which when activated by the customer requires immediate acknowledgment. After the initial purchase, the customers may believe that there is a standard of service that applies to distinct situations, this is just one example of an implied warranty. When activated, these warranties represent a specific form of company performance, and most important, a form of company appreciation for the customer's initial purchase.

The relationship created between service and the implied warranty determines whether the customer will continue to have a positive association with the company's brand. The strength of this relationship also determines whether the customer will buy other products of the same brand in the future.

The Solution Principles

The Monkey solution principles incorporate three service responsibility levels within the entire solution system.

- The overall service system assumes responsibility for all customer communications and provides consistent and continuous follow-through.
- The service system manages all customer communications from beginning to satisfactory conclusion.
- Whether or not the initial incident has been resolved, follow-through ensures that the highest standards are maintained for brand integrity and customer retention.

Monkey Chapter Overview

- Continuous civility is described as the relationship between customer loyalty and brand within the general product marketplace.
- Customers can be either individuals or groups who buy products or services, or both.
- Customers are classified as both internal and external.
- A fully responsive solution service system introduces continuous civility standards to establish the employee culture and code of conduct.
- The goal of the solution service system is to support customers and to manage customer retention.
- Managing continuous civility is the overall objective of a high-quality solution service system.
- Effective solutions offer customers alternative options, improve communication, and offer access to the company.
- Properly crafted solutions improve customer satisfaction and support the customer retention goals of the entire organization.

~ ~ ~

Chapter Eight

The Mission

"My mission starts at the core, the soul. It is felt in the heart and spoken through actions, not just words."

—Robert Kiyosaki

Mission Statement Trivia

One of the first mission statements originated with the popular American television series Star Trek.[5]

The business mission statement is described as the summary of purpose.

Monkey Culture

Company culture remains forever reliant on a standard of identity, which is interpreted through the behaviors of its employees. Without employees, there would be no brand identity to maintain and no reason to have a mission.

Purpose of the Company Mission

It would be interesting to find out if employees know their company's mission statement.

If they don't know, do they at least know where to find it? For example, is the mission statement easily located on the company web site or in the employee handbook? When was the last time any employee discussed the company's mission with someone else from the organization? Do employees know why the company mission statement exists, and even more important, how this statement of purpose applies to the scope of their responsibilities?

Designed for a Purpose

The mission statement introduces concrete business intentions, and these in turn produce clarity and direction for employees. Without these intentions, service agents and other employee work groups are placed in the precarious situation of making unqualified customer inquiry decisions. An unexpected outcome of unqualified inquiry decisions is the inability to identify opportunities that maximize the positioning of the company's brand.

Mission Destination

The Service Monkeys have observed that many company mission statements are often posted in obscure locations and not displayed in full view. Under these conditions, the statement of intention becomes trivialized and, more often than not, used mostly for public relations purposes.

Frequently, the mission statement decorates annual reports and other forms of customer correspondence. From being an active tool that demonstrates stability and solidarity, the mission statement is reduced to an irrelevant slogan.

The Target Zone

The Service Monkeys prefer that the mission statement decorate employee offices, recreation and other open-access work areas. These visible displays broadcast a continuous message of the company's purpose, ideals, and direction.

Within customer service, the mission of the company offers a reminder of superior service performance.

Monkey Mission

Employees who are not familiar with the mission and vision of their company may lag in performance standards. They may also exhibit a general lack of understanding of what their company's purpose is, and what each product or service represents within that purpose.

However, when companies offer training, which includes an understanding of the mission, this creates the foundation for a successful employee culture. The culture establishes a higher quality of overall service, and produces more opportunities for employees to increase company profits by promoting other products offered under the same brand.

A clear understanding and consistent use of the company's mission also offers direction, and encourages the entire employee culture to work toward the objectives that are identified by the statement of purpose.

Who Demands Service?

The answer to this question is: Every customer, both internal and external, deserves high-quality service.

Service quality extends beyond products and resources and should emulate the purpose of the company's mission statement.

One of the best examples of high-quality employee service delivery is provided by the concept "Leadership through Quality" (LQT), which was utilized in the early eighties by Xerox Corporation.[6]

CEO David T. Kearns and his senior management team used LQT to monitor customer satisfaction, making the maintenance of LQT standards the responsibility of every employee within the organization.

"Workers are vested with authority over day-to-day work decisions. And they are expected to take the initiative in identifying and correcting problems that affect the quality of products or services." (8a)

Unfortunately, LQT was never used by the business community at large. During the last two decades, a shrinking focus on employee training has resulted in fewer formal cultural standards and a heavy reliance on technology.

In all business situations, the employee culture is considered the foundation for high-quality customer satisfaction, and without reinforcing this culture, quality standards will suffer.

LQT describes customers as both internal and external. Within the company (known as internal), service delivery is the responsibility of all employees regardless of rank or position.

Outside the company (known as external), there are customers who may or may not purchase goods and services but will still require high-quality service. These customers include administrators and vendors who work with the organization.

Although certain divisions of the organization, such as sales, will have more direct exposure to customers, many internal employees may not have these same opportunities. By eliminating service distinctions (rank or position), service delivery becomes the responsibility of every employee within the organization.

These distinctions can be incorporated into the mission statement. The objectives become more attainable when the wording of the company's purpose identifies precise service delivery standards that include all customers, regardless of whether they are internal or external.

Monkey Roll Call: "Out of Sight, Out of Mind"

In an ever-changing business environment, the Service Monkeys encourage a continuous review of the mission statement.

The function of the company mission has a greater impact when it is spoken, heard, seen, and powerfully rooted in positive imagery. In contrast, when the mission statement is obscured, an unresponsive business environment is produced where the needs of employees, customers, shareholders, and its own innovations become diminished in value.

The elements of any mission may require adjustment so that they better serve both a changing business model and the product marketplace.

Mission Equals Service Delivery

The mission statement isolates the company's business purpose and interprets the standard of behavior of the employee culture.

A well-known example of a purpose intention is the American Pledge of Allegiance, which delivers a famous and evocative message of solidarity and idealism, practiced at the heart of American patriotism. In more concise terms, having a strong business purpose supports both the agreed standard of behavior and the organized employee culture.

The Service Monkeys prefer that the ideals of the mission statement be incorporated into all usual and customary business practices. This encourages organization-wide participation and delivers a higher standard of customer service.

Mission Statement = Established Employee Culture Combined with High-Quality Customer Service

Promoting the Mission

- Posting the mission—everywhere, in multiple and visible locations.
- Reciting the mission—at company events and meetings. If the mission only serves to embarrass, why have one?
- Advertising the mission—in appropriate marketing and promotional materials. This exposes customers to the company mission at every opportunity and promotes greater brand identity.
- The mission promotes loyalty within the employee culture; why not test employees on elements of the company mission as part of their evaluation?

Hiring with the Mission in Mind

The mission and the culture combined determine the caliber of employees who will lead the company to success.

Service standards are elevated when employees can articulate and communicate their company's mission.

Adhering to the mission statement becomes a continuous practice that yields two significant results: first, a higher service standard, and second, increased employee efficiency.

If the company mission is at the forefront of all hiring and other business practices, the entire organization becomes responsible for promoting successful customer interactions.

Employees Become the Mission

As it is stated, the company's mission identifies the role of all employees within that mission. If the mission represents the business purpose, employees are the greatest part of that purpose, and without their efforts, the mission cannot be achieved.

All divisions within the organization share the responsibility of upholding the mission. When employees are responsible for delivering high-quality service standards, they actively contribute to increasing positive business outcomes.

Monkey Divides

Within the business hierarchy when separate work groups coexist across product and service boundaries, successful communication is impaired throughout the organization. A hypothetical example of this occurs when there are five separate employee groups that deliver similar services within a single marketing organization. This represents five separate entities and not ABC Company—the organization.

When organizations are so large that combining work groups becomes challenging or too expensive, the result is poor customer retention and reduced revenue over time. Employee integration is preferred to produce fluid communication and unified goals, which embody the purpose of the mission statement.

Mission Exercise Questions

The following questions identify the goals and objectives of the mission statement. These questions presume that a mission statement already exists.

- How is your organization's purpose described in the company's mission statement?
- Does this purpose meet the needs of the entire organization as well as both internal and external customers?
- List any problems the company may be able to resolve by having a more precisely worded mission statement.
- What appears to be the primary purpose of the mission statement? Is there more than one purpose?
- Has this purpose changed since the mission statement was established?
- Does the company's purpose serve all three Monkey customer types? Describe how this is accomplished.
- How can the existing mission statement be reworded to include solution customer service and high-quality employee training?

Mission Exercise

Discuss the customer service mission and vision of FedEx as stated in their mission statement (see mission statement page 76). Identify the various components of service delivery and how these impact both internal and external customers.

Can the questions presented in the previous section also be answered by this mission statement?

Monkey Perfection

The following is FedEx's mission statement:

> FedEx will produce superior financial returns for shareowners by providing high value-added supply chain, transportation, business and related information services through focused operating companies. Customer requirements will be met in the highest quality manner appropriate to each market segment served. FedEx will strive to develop mutually rewarding relationships with its employees, partners and suppliers. Safety will be the first consideration in all operations. Corporate activities will be conducted to the highest ethical and professional standards.[7]

Monkey Chapter Overview

- The company culture is influenced by a predetermined standard of behavior. This standard emulates the purpose of the company.
- The mission statement is a guide that describes the company's purpose. This guide is used organization-wide to introduce high-quality business and service solutions, which serve both internal and external customers.
- The mission statement establishes the employee culture, instills a universal standard of organizational behavior, and

incorporates various solution systems that are used to offer customers high-quality service.

- Fully utilizing an intention-driven mission statement generates increased profits, improves business practices, and heightens brand recognition.
- The full impact of the company mission cannot be achieved without the cooperation and participation of all employees and business copartners.

~ ~ ~

Monkey Organizational Flow

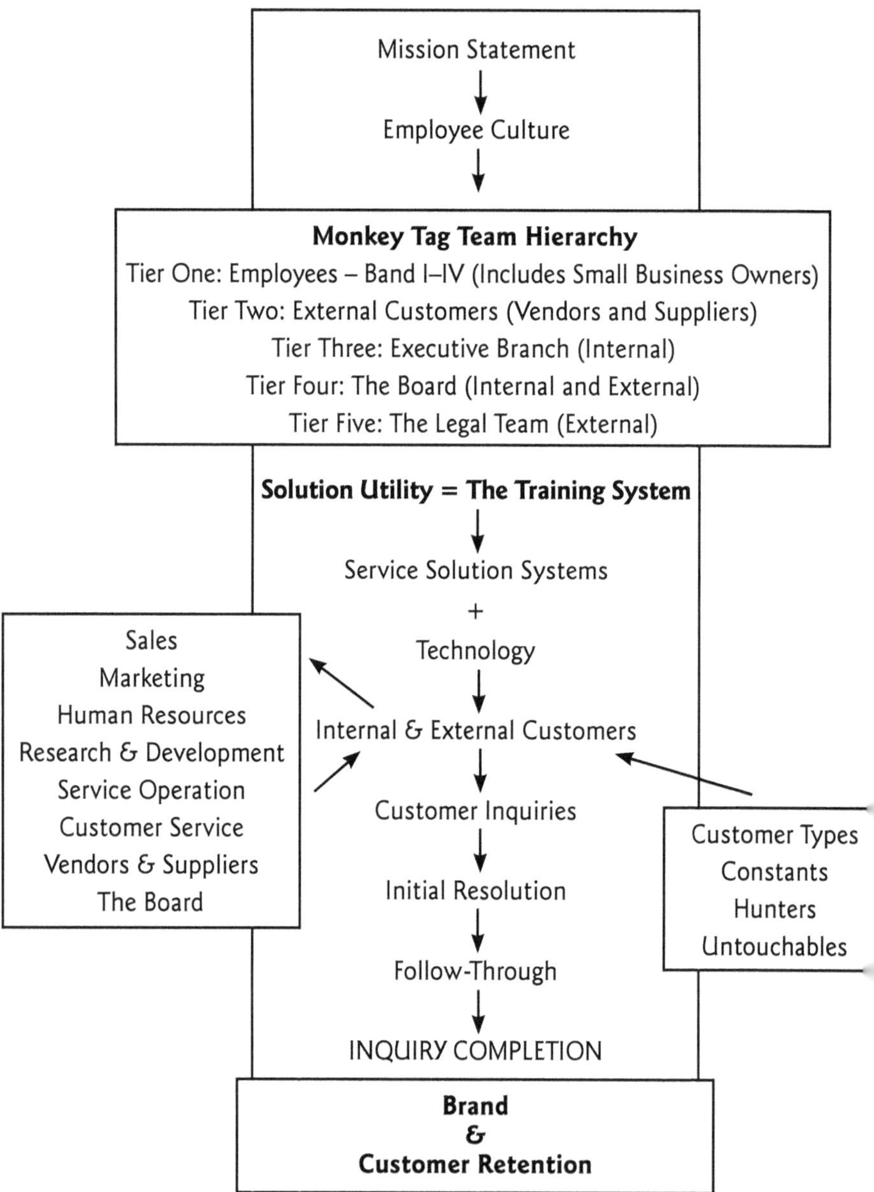

Chapter Nine

The Tag Team

"When you have disciplined people you don't need a hierarchy."

—Jim Collins, Good to Great

Monkey Definition

All Tag Teams contribute to high-quality service delivery.

The diagram below illustrates the structure of a Traditional Workforce Hierarchy.

Level Six: External Customers (Vendors & Suppliers)
Level Five: The Legal Team (External)
Level Four: The Board (Internal and External)
Level Three: The Executive Branch (Internal)
Level Two: Supervisors, Managers, or Small Business Owners (Internal)
Level One: Service Agents (Internal)

Monkey Tag Team Hierarchy

Monkeys in the wild do not exist in teams; they function as united groups or family clusters.

Tier One: Employees – Band I–IV (Includes Small Business Owners) (Internal)
Tier Two: External Customers (Vendors and Suppliers)
Tier Three: Executive Branch (Internal)
Tier Four: The Board (Internal and External)
Tier Five: The Legal Team (External)

Monkey Ideal

Resolving customer issues at their initial point of identification is a tier one activity. This is the initial point of customer contact and the most critical stage of service delivery.

Organizations that equip their tier one service agents with proactive inquiry solutions produce more successful outcomes than those service systems that offer a supervisory level.

Superior training produces service agents that have a higher inquiry resolution ratio and greater customer satisfaction incidents.

Monkey Chain of Resolution

The objective of a Monkey solution system is to resolve all customer inquiries to a satisfactory conclusion at their initial point of introduction. The large majority of inquiries are completed at the tier one stage of the organizational hierarchy.

Monitoring inquiries improves the overall system and increases both the quantity and quality of solutions offered.

Creating the Chain

The more service levels that exist in the organization's hierarchy, the more delays within the service resolution system.

The effectiveness of the Monkey hierarchy lies not in the number of agents available to handle service inquiries, but in the actual quality of solutions offered to resolve inquiries.

When tier one service agents resolve customer issues without supervisory intervention, the service delays are minimized and customer satisfaction improves. In that regard, the Service Monkeys consider the traditional supervisory level redundant.

Tracking customer responses can be a valuable indicator of service quality. For example, Hunters do not have the time or interest to deal with a complex organizational hierarchy. Their first concern is the expedient resolution of their inquiry, and second, how the organization delivers the standards of their own implied warranties.

Tier One Failure

What determines the intention of the solution system? Is the intention to supervise service agents or to manage customer inquiries, or to do both?

The primary role of a tier one service agent is to deliver high-quality customer solutions. Tier one service agents never manage other employees; they only manage customer inquiries.

Grading Systems

Band grading systems produce improved service agent responsiveness and higher incident resolution.

Band grading is hardly a new concept. Certain federal and local government agencies use band grading as part of their employee hiring and evaluation process. However, within the Monkey solution system band grading does not rely on tenure or years of service, but focuses on those standards of excellence that resolve service inquiries to completion and manage customer retention.

Over time, utilizing band systems can also improve employee retention and reduce continuous hiring and training expenses.

These band grading standards are established by using predetermined employee training programs and a complimentary evaluation process.

Managing Monkey Bands

Band grading management requires monitoring, and the monitoring standards are determined when the solution system is designed. These monitoring standards rely on several features, which include performance tracking tools, customer surveys, peer evaluations, and merit performance systems.

Band Structure

During a work shift, there may be several bands of employee experience represented. Having a variety of band experience improves service delivery and helps to manage the retention of all three customer types.

The highest band grade within each shift group represents the greatest level of solution experience. Although service agents may be trained to respond to most service scenarios, those who have achieved the highest band grade are considered mentors and can perform other work activities such as training support and special service projects.

Monkey Chapter Overview

- There may be many service tag teams within the solution system. Examples of tag teams include the unified efforts of direct sales, operations, billing, and accounting, which will each have service tiers of employees at varying band grades.
- The service tag team is comprised of mixed values of customer service knowledge and solution experience.
- Tier one is the most influential level within the tag team and has the most experience when it comes to customer retention and promoting brand integrity. Tier one provides solutions to customers at the initial point of interaction.
- The traditional supervisory level is not considered vital to the tag team because this role cannot contribute to managing customer retention or elevating brand recognition.
- The role of the supervisor interrupts service flow because supervisors may also be required to manage other employees.

~ ~ ~

The Say Monkey always promotes effective communication.

Say communication supports all customer types, both internal and external.

Say communication is always solution-driven and focuses on resolving customer issues at the initial point of contact.

The purpose of Say communication is to improve customer relations while elevating the importance of the company's brand.

Chapter Ten

Why the Customer Always Wins

"The human species is unique because it alone can create, recognize and exercise options. It is part of human uniqueness that we are endowed with the faculty of choice."

—Norman Cousins

Monkey Influence

Customers always have a choice where to buy products and services.

A customer's power to influence affects the entire organizational culture, from product performance to service delivery. A higher standard of service delivery is vital when a company's brand becomes vulnerable to the competition.

Any customer inquiry that is not resolved to completion indirectly stimulates competition and negatively impacts customer retention.

Competition is often more influential in economies of developed nations, such as the United States and Western Europe, where there are multiple versions of the same products and services.

Having a vast array of choices becomes amplified in a competitive arena, particularly when that competitive arena expands to global markets. For example, when the choices appear to be endless, consumers can opt to buy either an American-made product or a Korean-made product. They can also buy the original brand or a generic version that may be less expensive.

In contrast, less developed countries have fewer purchasing options, which reduces the need for high-quality customer service.

Unusual Service Meltdown

During the last decade, American ingenuity can be symbolized as the sacrificial lamb of the global economy. Specific to the automobile industry, the purchase of an American car has been influenced by such conditions as climate change, aesthetics, fuel efficiency, a lack of quality standards, inefficient warranties, depreciating product value, and, let's not forget, below-standard customer service.

The U.S. Census Bureau reported that in both 2006 and 2007 Michigan was the only state in which the poverty rate climbed.[8] The widespread economic impacts of 9/11, coupled with a gradual decline in the American automobile industry, resulted in a loss of jobs and the displacement of workers.

In recent years, American consumers have been less impressed by the promotional "bells and whistles" that are sold with American cars. The focus has been on value and higher service standards. Reliability and cost of ownership have also played significant roles in the final purchase decision.

Foreign-Made

The Japanese automobile industry has been able to cater to all of these consumer demands while offering a wide variety of fuel-efficient automobiles that are less expensive to maintain over time. From basic utility to adequate luxury, Japanese vehicles have not always been considered aesthetically pleasing but more functional and efficient. In addition, Japanese-made cars enjoy a higher standard of overall performance, which is supported by value and brand integrity. Most consumers, particularly Constants, have been drawn to the superior service warranties of the mid-sized and mid-priced vehicles, which make them more often than not repeat customers. The growing number of Hunters ensures that the greatest number of future car purchases will be based on value.

What Has Shifted?

When products are no longer manufactured in the United States, American consumers will be less inclined to buy American brands, particularly when most (if not all) of the components that make up these "American" products are manufactured in other parts of the world. Figure 10-1 illustrates a hypothetical example of these new buying trends. Where two computers are identically manufactured, brand is the only factor that justifies price.

Computer Brand A
Branded by American company Y.
Components made by foreign company X.
Manufactured by foreign company X.
Cost $1000.

Identical Computer Brand B
Branded by foreign company X.
Components made by foreign company X.
Manufactured by foreign company X.
Cost $750.

Figure 10-1. Hypothetical Buying Dynamics.

In the above example, brand is the only commodity that can survive beyond manufacturing. The brand placement of a product improves when it is combined with the promise of a high-quality warranty and superior service.

Global Consequences

The outsourcing of U.S. manufacturing jobs to overseas markets has produced an unexpected deterioration of American brand integrity.

In the previous example, consumers are not affected by where the computers are manufactured. However, manufacturing overseas does increase competition, which does impact brand because it allows consumers to consider foreign vendors.

Consumer Response

In the automobile example, when carmakers offer superior warranties, which are supported by high-quality service standards, the consumer investment continues to perform regardless of a shift in economic trends. Offering superior service manages market share and customer loyalty. If the prevailing economy trends lower, the quality of the brand has already determined the buying standard. An example of this is the story of a computer company that experienced reduced market share in the nineties during a period of less product development. The quality of the brand survived over a long period of poor revenue performance and was resurrected when new products were introduced over a decade later. The most interesting aspect of this story is that the initial computer product was never abandoned. The combined influence of customer loyalty and sustained brand performance supported the old technologies until they could be improved and reintroduced to the same loyal customer base.

Service Quality

After the initial product purchase, the service warranty, when executed, must match what has been explicitly offered.

For a brand to survive, service solutions must also be of an impeccably high standard.

Intangible products such as insurance require an even higher standard of performance because the implied warranty may or may not be executed. When there is a poor standard of compliance, or if there is a change in terms, the integrity of the brand is impacted.

Customer Warranty Appreciation

Each Monkey customer type also influences market change. When an influx of complimentary products creates excessive competition, the number of customer types in the service hourglass fluctuates.

As competition increases, Constants become a diminishing customer type. Service solution systems work to retain Constants because this customer type is loyal to the brand and will more than likely be a repeat customer. In addition, there is less marketing expense required to retain Constants.

Hunters are expensive to manage and maintain. Because Hunters have no brand loyalty, their numbers will fluctuate. How a company offers marketing incentives will affect the number of Hunters in the service hourglass.

If customer retention continues to fluctuate, large and iconic companies will struggle to maintain their marketplace influence, particularly if the products they manufacture and distribute are disposable or rely on changing technology.

Monkey Chapter Overview

- Global economic change influences consumer buying trends.
- Brand performance deteriorates when there is excessive competition.
- Retaining higher levels of Constants will help to manage greater revenue performance over time.
- Constants are the most valued customer type because they are loyal to brand and are repeat buyers.
- The more competition, the greater the need for high-quality customer service to manage brand integrity and product market share.
- The number of product purchases is influenced by brand recognition, a customer's perception of the product's value, where it is manufactured, and where it is sold.

~ ~ ~

Chapter Eleven

Service Templates: The Destroyers!

"The professional in contrast to the amateur. Consider the differences. The amateur plays for fun, the professional plays for keeps."

—Steven Pressfield, *The War of Art*

Service Definition

Technology serves to replace creative thinking and regulate human behavior.

Service templates are technology and process driven. Service templates cannot be customized to meet specific customer needs. The efficiency of a static service template is determined by the inventor of the template, who may or may not be familiar with the individual service needs of the customers served or the purpose of the company's mission.

Technology Interruptions

The present service environment has produced a human reliance on short-term technologies. For example, the availability of cash registers and calculators no longer require any thinking skills to process simple calculations. Also, many keypad technologies now offer access to changing information such as flight reservations and credit card balances. For accuracy, these technologies require continuous support and monitoring.

Technology also places the burden of understanding on the consumer's ability to operate each technology system.

Monkey Reminder

Within Monkey service systems, templates are considered a support technology and not a service delivery solution.

The Service Monkeys describe technology as a secondary support tool that assists service agents in delivering inquiry solutions.

Superior customer service is a by-product of creative human ingenuity that never relies on technology.

Monkey Dialogue

The following is a short dialogue between Service Agent John and his customer Jane. The purpose of this dialogue is to illustrate how solution systems deliver customized options using technology templates.

Service Agent: Hello, this is John. Thank you for calling XYZ. May I ask your name?
Customer: My name is Jane.
Service Agent: Hello, Jane. On behalf of XYZ, how can I help you?
Customer: I would like to know why I was charged a late charge.
Service Agent: Jane, can I have your account number?

...

Service Agent: Jane, I see here we received your payment after the due date.
Customer: I understand that, John, but I have been a loyal customer and this is my first ever late charge.
Service Agent: Jane, our records indicate that XYZ adjusted late fees as a courtesy on your account two months ago. Unfortunately, we are unable to reverse a second late fee.
Customer: John, I've been having problems receiving my mail because of the post office. As you can see by my records, I usually always pay on time, but as I said, there was a problem with my mail.
Service Agent: Yes, Jane, I understand, and I appreciate your loyalty, but we are unable to make the adjustment because of the prior incident two months ago. However, I can offer you two options. First, if you make your

payments continuously for the next twelve months, we can reverse this late charge on the thirteenth month. With the second option, you can submit your inquiry in writing to our customer resolution department, and they will research the situation further.

Customer: I see, John. Well, I will take option one for the moment, but if I am not happy with the decision, I will write a letter.

Service Agent: I will go ahead and make a note on your file. The adjustment will be made automatically on the thirteenth month, unless, of course, you decide to write a letter. I will also go ahead and send you a notice outlining the adjustment requirements. Do you have a pen available? I can give you the address if you change your mind and decide to write.

Service Agent: Jane, as you know, XYZ values your loyalty, so I would like to present you with another option. We offer a late fee reduction program. The cost is $30.00; this is an annual fee. If for any reason you are late in the future, your late fees are automatically reduced by fifty percent. Does this option interest you?

Customer: Not really, John. I plan on not being late again.

Service Agent: You can call anytime to add this option to your account. Is there anything else I can help you with?
Customer: No, thank you, John.
Service Agent: If you have further questions, please feel free to call us again. It has been my pleasure to help you today.

~ ~ ~

Monkey Review

In this example, the service agent offers three customized service options. He also manages to mention the company name four times, which serves to elevate brand identity.

One of the service options that was offered is commonly refered to as an "up-sell." This is an opportunity for the company to introduce new products and services and thereby create an indirect revenue stream.

Finally, this scenario could be viewed as a company "win" situation. The company's solution retained Jane as a customer. John, realizing that Jane was a Constant, offered a value-added product versus a discount or incentive. No revenue was lost, and Jane remained satisfied with the solutions John offered.

Monkey Chapter Overview

- Technology-driven templates hinder the delivery of creative service agent solutions.

- Within generic service systems, reduced profitability and brand recognition is attributed to the overuse of technology templates.
- Using technology templates negatively impacts the company's mission, brand, and reputation because technology cannot always offer the appropriate solutions.
- Technology templates are static process systems that cannot be customized to meet specific customer service issues.
- An overuse of technology discounts employee training and encourages a greater reliance on redundant and static service templates.
- Static templates are considered ineffective when it comes to delivering service solutions, which are required to manage customer retention and brand longevity.

~ ~ ~

Chapter Twelve

You Are Going to Transfer Me Where?

"When it comes to taking care of your best customers, be creative."

—Robert Kiyosaki

Phone Service

The Service Monkeys are not in favor of transferring customers. Transferring calls is simply another way of saying, "Sorry, I don't know how to help you. Let me find someone who can."

Transferring customer calls suggests that the service being offered is inferior and service agents are unable to respond to customer issues because they are untrained. This also indicates that the organization does not value its customers enough to invest in employee training; they do, however, invest in redundant static technologies.

Technology Limitations

When the service system relies heavily on phone trees and other technologies to manage customer inquiries, the customer satisfaction standard diminishes. Transferring options, as well as multiple transfer situations, initiates unnecessary customer frustration and overall service dissatisfaction.

Solution System Requirements

The amount of service agent training offered is determined by the size, distribution, and responsibilities of each work group within the entire solution system. The more direct customer communication offered, the more training required to support the already established standards of service interaction.

Within the solution service system, the training standard also determines the success of brand longevity.

One Size Fits All?

Would a customer be surprised to hear the following statement? "Sorry, I'm uncertain what to do in this particular situation. I really would like to help you, but I need to investigate your inquiry further to find a better solution."

It is often assumed that the existing service system can resolve all types of customer inquiries. Special inquiry conditions may require more time for resolution, and customers must be receptive to unavoidable delays after which they may receive a more favorable outcome.

Delayed responses are preferred over being transferred within the phone tree system with the hopes of finding someone in the organization who can resolve the inquiry.

Service Dialogue Senario

The following two-part dialogue introduces a service scenario that addresses how technology-driven solutions are often ineffective when they cannot be customized.

Static Template: Part One

Service Agent: My name is Lisa. How can I help you today?
Customer: Well, I'm relieved I finally got through to someone. Do you have any idea how many buttons I had to push on my phone before I reached you? Your phone system also cut me off twice, and I had no clue which button to push to get the help I needed.
Service Agent: I'm sorry to hear that. I will make sure the problem is investigated. What can I do to help you?
Customer: I haven't received a statement for three months. To be honest, I forgot all about it, and I will probably have some late fees, which I will have to pay. The only question I have is, why haven't I been receiving my bills?

Service Agent: Do you happen to know your account number?

Customer: Yes, here it is ...

...

Service Agent: It looks like your mail was returned to us.

Customer: But I personally called and changed my address after I opened my account.

Service Agent: Is your address 123 Street, zip code 00003?

Customer: The zip code is wrong. It should be 00033. I told the other service agent this when I first opened my account. I live in a newly constructed housing development, and some databases have not been updated to reflect the new zip codes. I told that person to enter the zip code carefully and then check it.

Service Agent: I will be happy to change it now.

Customer: Please make sure the zip code is right after you press enter. Also, I don't think it's fair that I pay the late fees because I did call to correct my address. As I said before, from the first billing period the zip code has been wrong.

> **Service Agent:** Your account indicates $80.00 in late fees plus the past-due amount for all three delinquent months.
> **Customer:** I really don't think I should have to pay all those late fees because I did call to change my address.
> **Service Agent:** I'm sorry; I tried, but my system won't let me reverse the charges. It looks like you will have to pay them.
> **Customer:** I want to speak to a supervisor.
> **Service Agent:** Of course, please hold for one moment while I transfer you.

...

In this example, the customer has several concerns.

- Not being able to manage the phone tree system.
- Not receiving statements.
- Being charged excessive late fees.
- The late fees cannot be reversed.
- The past-due amount is still outstanding.

Although the service agent has corrected the address, the customer has exhausted all of the solutions at this service tier and the static template cannot be customized. Also, the template was not designed to accept new zip codes unless they are manually entered, and it cannot issue a full credit for the $80 in late fees.

At the very beginning of the call, the customer had problems managing the phone tree and now the customer has been transferred to a supervisor.

Most important, this situation was not created by the customer. He or she is already dissatisfied with the level of service being offered, as well as the inefficiency of the service system.

The quality of the brand has been diminished, and the customer remains unhappy.

The company has made a total of $80 in artificial late fees and in the process has lost the customer's respect, which impacts brand recognition.

Static Template: Part Two

The scene continues. The customer has complained and has requested to be transferred to the supervisory level.

Supervisor: Hello! My name is John. I understand you are disputing the late fees on your account.
Customer: Well, I don't think I should have to pay late fees when I provided your company with my correct address.
Supervisor: But you are responsible for paying your bills on time.
Customer: And I would have done that if I had received my bills. There have been problems with the address from the first month when I was forced to pay my bill without a statement. After I called to change the address, I thought the problem had been corrected. For a few months, I received my

bills on time, but that was only because the post office was forwarding my mail. I've now been informed that the address is still wrong. I explained all of this to the first service agent months ago. That person told me that they had corrected my address, but apparently that didn't happen.

Supervisor: We input the address from the original contracts you signed.

Customer: Well, whoever put in the information did it incorrectly.

Supervisor: Let me pull up a copy of your documents.

Customer: You can do that?

Supervisor: Yes, everything is scanned and downloaded into our system. It will take a few moments.

Customer: Another thing I'm concerned about is my credit. Now I have delinquent billing and late fees.

Supervisor: Let me try to take care of this issue first. Yes, here are your documents now.

...

It would appear that the address was not put into our system correctly. I'm very sorry for the inconvenience.

Customer: What will you do?

Supervisor: Well, the zip code issue has now been corrected. I can send an e-mail to our processing department and ask them to reverse the late fees and correct anything that may negatively impact your credit history.

Customer: Thank you. Now, what should I do to make my payments current?

Supervisor: I'm sorry; my system does not accept payments. I have to transfer you to another department.

Monkey Review

This happens to be a true story.

The positive outcome is that the zip code has been finally corrected. Also, an e-mail has been sent to the processing department requesting a reversal of the late fees and adjustment to the customer's credit history to remove any negative incidents.

At the conclusion of the second part of this call, the customer has still not paid his or her bill or received a correct invoice; instead, he or she is transferred again to another service division to process the payment.

The company has lost revenue, wasted manpower hours, and diminished the value of their brand. They have also invested in redundant technologies that cannot be managed by the customers or the employees that they serve.

Monkey Review Questions

- What outcomes would have changed if the level-one service agent had been given access to the same system, training, and resources as the supervisor?
- What are the service flow issues created by the static technologies and the phone tree?
- What are the negative impacts on customer satisfaction?
- In your opinion, would this customer choose to do business with this company again? Does he or she have other options? What are these options?
- What, in your opinion, is the time line for this customer (meaning the estimated time that the customer will continue to do business with this company)?

Monkey Chapter Overview

- Within Monkey solution systems, transferring the customer is viewed as a brand inhibitor.
- The continued use of poorly planned phone trees and other static technologies affect brand longevity over time.
- High-quality service agent training elevates brand integrity and long-term customer retention. Training also improves the quality of inquiry solutions, allowing tier one service agents to complete inquiry resolution at the initial point of customer contact.

~ ~ ~

Chapter Thirteen

Web Solutions?

"It's not what you say, it's how you prepare for the day."

—Robert Kiyosaki

The Best Monkey Tool

Would any company substitute their CEO and frontline management for technology?

No one can argue that automation has produced a dynamic shift in how we do business and how we view employment. During the last decade, the use of technology has impacted all aspects of global life, from buying a car to finding a romantic partner. Along the way, adjustments have been made to improve technology efficiency, which has allowed greater access to a valuable and cost-savings tool.

As one example of advanced technology use, the Internet has changed how customers receive service solutions. The most unsatisfactory of these outcomes has been the overuse of the Internet, which has eliminated the need for the traditional human service interface.

The use of e-mail is a form of technology that is widely used as a substitute for direct human customer retention. When used as a static template, e-mail fails as a customer retention communication device. The static format can only adapt to the prevailing business conditions and cannot be customized.

In addition, the expanded use of e-mail has accelerated the "quickening" response (discussed earlier). This has required faster but not necessarily more efficient methods of customer inquiry resolution.

Service System Planning

Modern employee recruitment practices serve as an example of how the Internet impacts company productivity by limiting creative participation.

Recruitment as a process could be compared to fitting a wet suit on a seal, the unique process used for selecting qualified candidates being the cornerstone to building and maintaining the employee culture of the organization.

During the last decade, many large companies have resorted to using the Internet as a primary recruitment screening tool. Candidates are evaluated based on a series of Internet interactions, from the submission of résumés to candidate testing and elimination. The effectiveness of this tool is determined by the candidate's ability to follow the technology instructions.

The Service Monkeys agree that the Internet is a useful tool for fielding applications. During the early recruitment stages, the static process collects information based on predetermined criteria. However, depending on design features, these systems cannot be relied upon to fully interpret candidate qualifications.

Static templates also produce a range of generic responses, from the acknowledgment that is sent when the candidate's application is received to the acknowledgment that delivers a polite "no, thank you, but we appreciate your interest."This last acknowledgment is usually delivered when the candidate does not meet the preset qualification criterion.

Because templates produce generic responses, when these templates are poorly planned, they fail to meet their intended purpose. The outcome is an inefficient service system that generates negative perceptions of the company and how it values its customers.

As a final note, because many Constants show less interest in the Internet, recruitment results maybe inconsistent, and this will impact the service outcomes for the entire organization and its mission.

Monkey Outcomes

Other than the initial e-mail contact, template communications should be kept to a minimum. Other preferred forms of service communication include personal phone calls, handwritten notes, and personalized form letters. Finally, any correspondence that uses company letterhead elevates the importance of the message that is being delivered.

Monkey Web

The World Wide Web is useful for gathering and sharing information. The company Web site is a tool that should provide customers with business contact information, service phone numbers, and the correspondence mailing address. This is essential to establishing improved communication and open access.

Monkey Associations

Customers may not identify a company by its use of technology. This also applies to computer and technology companies that may sell computers but are run by an employee culture.

Customers do, however, identify a company by its brand, as well as any implied and expressed warranties. The brand is associated with the quality of service delivery. If the technology used by the service system does not meet basic functioning requirements, then it will not meet the service expectations of the customer. The brand and the company are connected to the service system by the customer's overall perceptions of how employees manage his or her inquiries.

The purpose of any service tool, particularly the Internet, is to perform an identified function—offering a simplistic example, a hammer pounds and scissors cut or stab. The Internet as a tool can accept candidate résumés and acknowledge predetermined recruitment activities by using e-mail at various stages of the recruitment process.

Monkey Technology Tools

The following technology tools when properly designed also support solution systems.

The Acknowledgment

This tool is used to respond to "usual and customary" service activities. The acknowledgment represents immediate customer appreciation and brand recognition. The acknowledgment is always automatic and contains a static message. Examples include form letters and e-mails that offer a generic response.

Notifications

These are used for follow-up and to verify information. For example, a notice may include a tracking number for a unique purchase.

Thank-You

The only Service Monkey rule is that a thank-you must be sent. The thank-you officially notifies the customer that his or her order is appreciated. The thank-you promotes brand integrity and customer appreciation.

Web Surveys

As it pertains to the entire service system, feedback is critical to improving service delivery. In order to be fully effective, Web surveys should be no more than three to eight questions in length. Most important, these questions focus on a variety of topics such as the pre-call purchase experience, service proficiency, and warranty performance.

Improving survey participation becomes an indirect goal of the survey and may include the following considerations:

- The survey data collected will mean more to the company than to the customer.
- Usually the survey will be delivered post sales or post service. Note: The type of survey issued (mail or E-mail) directs the level of response based on the customer type.
- Survey efficiency may require offering incentives in the form of future percentage discounts, coupon savings, or special offers, which entice customers (Hunters) to complete more accurate survey information.

Web Credit Card Payments

All credit card purchases must be acknowledged. The most immediate and cost-effective method is by using e-mail acknowledgments.

Other Service Communication Tools

Unusual situations may require other forms of static communication. These solution tools includes:

- Acknowledgments that specifically respond to customer letters or other inquiries.
- Acknowledgments that inform—for example, letters that include a follow-up date if further action is pending for an open inquiry.
- Acknowledgments that provide tracking numbers for service inquiries that need further investigation.

Monkey Chapter Overview

- Technology was never designed as a means to an end.
- There are limited situations in which the Internet and other technologies can be used to replace effective human interactions and proficient communication.
- The Internet is a static response technology, which is not suitable for primary service communications.
- When the Internet is used for business, sufficient planning is required to integrate this tool so that it achieves the predetermined objective.
- Internet recruitment is never an entire solution, but a single component of the entire recruitment system.
- Internet communication during the recruitment process may include the following:
    - A thank-you to all candidates. This acknowledgment includes the company's mission statement and any message relating to the company's overall hiring goals.
    - A follow-up acknowledgment, which describes any future recruitment activities that may affect the candidate.
    - A letter of regret sent to candidates who do not meet the position requirements.
- Voice-over-Internet protocol (VoIP) is a new and inexpensive Internet technology. Voice-activated acknowledgments can offer recruitment messages at various stages of the recruitment process. These voice messages can be created by the head of the recruitment division and delivered to candidates who have provided contact phone numbers.

~ ~ ~

Chapter Fourteen

Solutions in Motion

"Problem Solvers know that if they can accurately state the cause of a problem, they have taken a giant step toward solving it."

—Paul W. Swets

Customer Appreciation

A timely response to customer inquiries is the most significant form of appreciation.

Open access to customer service is critical to the complete resolution of customer inquiries.

Monkey Exercise

Consider the service options presented in the following solution scenario and then answer the questions at the end of the section.

Service Agent: Hello, my name is John. How can I help you today?
Customer: I am unable to attend a class I have registered for. The next class is twelve months away, and I can't wait that long. I need to cancel my registration.
Service Agent: I'm sorry to hear that. This happens to be an excellent course.
Customer: Yes, I agree; however, I can't take the class right now, and I would like my tuition refunded.
Service Agent: I'm sure I can find a solution. I should mention that there is a $100 cancellation fee.
Customer: That doesn't seem fair.
Service Agent: I understand; however, that's the policy for this particular course.
Customer: I still don't think that's very fair. I had every intention of attending, but this course is only offered once a year.
Service Agent: Is there another course you might like to take?
Customer: Well, I did consider course B, but it is out of my price range.
Service Agent: If your schedule permits, I can offer you course B at this year's prices. You will be able to apply all the money you have already paid from the course you are canceling and not incur the cancellation fee.

I can also offer you an installment plan to pay for the difference in price.

Customer: You mean I will pay this year's prices and not lose my $100?

Service Agent: Yes.

Customer: Wow! I know how expensive this course is. Using installments, I can afford the class and not lose the cancellation fee. Yes, I would like to do that.

Monkey Questions

- Identify the customer's issues in this scenario.
- List the customer's original complaint(s).
- List the service agent's solutions and match these solutions to each of the customer's complaints.
- Within the service system that exists at your organization, what do customers ask for that cannot be delivered immediately?
- What creative solutions would you add to resolve the issues you listed above?
- List potential solutions that might allow you to improve the level of service you currently offer to your customers.

Exercise Review

The solutions offered in this scenario are effective because they allow the service agent to negotiate in the company's best interest.

The only other option for this customer would be to receive a refund of the initial tuition, minus the $100 cost for canceling the course.

This solution created a win-win situation. The customer continued to do business with the company. The final service outcome also produced an unanticipated revenue stream, which maintained class enrollment and increased fees. Most significant, the options maintained a high level of customer satisfaction and at the same time elevated brand identity.

Monkey Brand

Solution customer service focuses on managing brand identity. As a reminder, before customers buy anything, most already have other options as to where they can purchase similar goods and services. Whenever the brand is elevated, this produces positive associations between the company and its customers.

Monkey Service Levels

The following are three descriptions of service levels that impact the customer's perception of brand. These service levels also influence competition.

Service Level: Monkey Zero—

No human interaction is offered. Customer service is fully automated by technology, which may cause the customer to arrive at "service dead ends."

Within the Monkey solution system, these situations are viewed as unsatisfactory because they ignore brand placement and allow customers to consider competitive vendors.

At the zero level, technology is used to deliver information that must be closely monitored for accuracy. The information options include payments received and balances due.

Service Level: Monkey One—Maintenance with No Up-Sell Provisions

This level represents 100 percent template service. Service agents receive basic training and do not provide service beyond the static template. This level also relies on supervisors to resolve more complex customer inquiries.

Monkey One increases in cost over time because technology must be updated and replaced.

Whenever service supervisors are added to the service hierarchy, this produces a duplication of service delivery, which results in unnecessary customer frustration. Monkey One always undervalues customer retention and brand.

Service Level: Monkey Two—Full-Solution Model

Monkey Two is the optimum service choice.

Phone trees are designed with a maximum of three phone prompts before a customer reaches a trained customer service agent.

Monkey Two agents vary in tenure and experience. The distribution of Monkey Two agents will vary throughout the service organization. This combination of knowledge and experience covers a wide variety of solutions, which serves to support all three Monkey customer types. Monkey Two agents have also been trained to promote and sell other products and services.

Other Solutions

Within all solution systems, employees and specifically service agents are responsible for identifying solution options and resolving customer inquiries to completion.

The variety of solutions will vary based on the type of inquiries, product upgrades, and customer incentives offered.

If the solutions do not meet the customers' expectations, they can elevate their inquiries in writing to an administrative support organization. Tracking numbers are assigned to monitor inquiries that require further investigation and follow-up.

Service Agent Incentives

Solution service agents never receive commissions as part of their compensation, unless they are directly employed by a sales organization.

Service performance is evaluated by the number of products and upgrades sold, as well as the overall improvement in customer satisfaction within the work group.

The standards for employee evaluation are predetermined by the company and are reviewed regularly. These standards are determined using a combination of tools and resources, which include customer survey responses and letters of appreciation.

Customer Rewards

Often inquiry solutions are designed by each service organization before the solution system is implemented. Solutions are administered by employees who have specialized training and sufficient knowledge to maintain the company's rigorous service standards.

The following are suggested solution examples. They may not apply to all companies or product situations but can be augmented when necessary.

- Company credits, which can be used to purchase future services and products.
- Special refunds, which are issued only if circumstances warrant or when there are uncommon service conditions.
- Reversal of service fees. This is a courtesy and cannot be repeated more than once within any calendar year.
- Upgrades to other products. Using the previous course tuition example, the customer risked losing $100 if he or she did not accept the upgrade option.
- Change of billing cycle, or offering customized payment options.
- A future service discount. For example, a customer originally paid $25 and now receives a $30 reward credit. This credit can be used over a predetermined period toward another purchase, and is offered only when the company is at fault or has provided a poor level of service.
- Coupons used for future discounts. These are applied as a reward when the customer upgrades his or her product or service.
- Graduated discounts. For example, the addition of a new phone feature such as call waiting, which may usually cost

an extra $5 per month, is now offered at $3 per month for a twelve-month term.

- A partial refund based on time lapsed. For example, the original contract was for twelve months, but the customer only used four. He or she now receives a credit for eight months or the balance of the contract term.
- The opportunity for someone at the executive level to offer other solutions. This option is discouraged, particularly when complete customer resolution is preferred at the initial point of contact (Tier one).
- The customer's inquiry needs further investigation. This situation is the least favorable because it will extend the resolution time; however, under certain conditions, it may be necessary.

Monkey Exercise

Which customer upgrades and alternative incentives are offered by your company? List all options that may or may not be available at this time. These options should be win-win situations and never compromise customer retention, company brand, revenue, or any other service support system within the organization.

Monkey Chapter Overview

- The first solution rule is timely responses to all customer inquiries.
- Within Monkey solution systems, service delivery compliments the company's customer appreciation process.
- There are three levels of service delivery from Monkey Zero to the Full-Solution Model.

~ ~ ~

The Do Monkey improves service delivery by adapting solutions to include promotions and incentives.

Do activities resolve customer inquiries and manage customer retention.

Chapter Fifteen

Monkey Follow-Through

"You can if you think you can."
—Norman Vincent Peale

Monkey Promise

Service promises are not representative of follow-through unless they are fully executed.

Following through is critical to high-quality service delivery.

Why critical? Because follow-through results in elevated brand performance and improved customer retention.

Follow-through also represents the company's commitment to resolving customer issues by offering complete solutions.

The purpose of follow-through is to manage customer retention by elevating customer satisfaction.

Follow-through cannot be fully executed unless employees have the skills and knowledge to administer complete inquiry solutions. In concert with direct service inquiry resolution, high-quality and continuous employee training are effective tools that can be used to manage and monitor continuous follow-through.

Monkey Integrity

Within Monkey solution systems, follow-through is a standard of organizational behavior. When follow-through standards are neglected, the entire organization is affected, from sales to service delivery and service support.

Follow-Through Tools

Most static technology service systems rely on e-mail to provide follow-through.

Although e-mail can be effective for certain forms of acknowledgment, letter-style formats should be viewed as an incomplete form of customer communication because they rely on the predictable wording of a static template.

In certain situations, e-mail will not meet the service requirements for each customer type. For example, Constants will be less likely to value e-mail notifications because they already appreciate the company's brand. In contrast, Hunters only appreciate e-mail communications when they include some sort of incentive.

Because e-mail correspondence cannot be guaranteed, e-mail follow-through is considered as secondary to direct, in-person communication.

Service Responsibility

Although every employee working within a solution system is charged with delivering high-quality service outcomes, the greatest responsibility for follow-through rests with service agents whose principal activity is service delivery.

Solution-trained service agents deliver inquiry resolutions based on predetermined service goals created by the organization, and supported by the mission statement, revenue objectives, and customer retention standards.

Follow-through is always dependent upon how the solution system is designed. A solution system can anticipate common inquiry outcomes and produce the appropriate solutions. Those inquiries that do not meet the predetermined criteria are resolved using customized solutions.

The primary goal of follow-through is to resolve customer inquiries at the initial point of introduction and always to completion.

Follow-Through Flow Systems

Inquiry flow is always monitored by the organization because the type of customer inquiries will vary based on where they originate and how they are resolved.

Company-designed measurement tools can monitor the performance of the system as well as any adjustments that are required to maintain performance standards. These measurement tools also identify when the system requires improvement or augmentation.

The Process

Whenever resolutions of customer inquiries require investigation and research, delivering complete solutions may be delayed. In these situations, incident software can manage the follow-through process by adjusting the status of pending customer inquiries. This software can be designed so it updates resolution dates, the inquiry status, and also the flow of e-mail notifications. This continuity helps to keep customers informed about the various stages of resolution for their inquiries.

Monkey Sales

The number of customer inquiries received will depend upon the number of services and products sold.

The more products available for purchase, the more service agents will be needed to manage customer retention and service delivery standards. Combining employee training and tenure bands can regulate the number of inquiries over time.

Monkey Chapter Overview

- The term follow-through implies dedicated attention to both customer service inquiries and company performance standards.
- Effective follow-through is critical to company stability because it promotes customer retention.
- Follow-through mirrors the company's overall commitment to resolving customer issues. A lack of consistent follow-through indicates a lapse in the company's observation of its mission.
- When there are multiple service systems that support one organization, the processes that manage follow-through are predetermined by the company and emulate the purpose of the mission statement.

- All follow-through processes are supported by high-quality employee training.
- Unless the customer inquiry is resolved to completion, follow-through becomes a continuous activity.
- A lack of service follow-through negatively impacts brand integrity and customer retention over time.

~ ~ ~

Chapter Sixteen

Gift Days

"Appreciation is a wonderful thing: It makes what is excellent in others belong to us as well."
—Francois Marie Arouet (Voltaire)

Unexpected Service Solutions

In the United States, Valentine's Day has become a tradition similar to Christmas, Easter, and Thanksgiving. These and many other events require participating in rituals and celebrations that encourage various forms of gift-giving.

Another reason why these events are considered special is because they represent a moment when everyday routines require increased human interaction and communication.

By using deliberate marketing and promotional activities, service delivery can also produce gift-giving opportunities and rituals. These activities can manage brand and stimulate new streams of revenue.

Celebrating Solutions

Solutions that embrace promotions produce win-win situations and promote elevated brand recognition. Offering incentives also introduces opportunities to accumulate valuable data, which helps to monitor customer retention and manage the customer types that enter and leave the service hourglass.

The goal of these incentives is to introduce a form of customer appreciation that continues well beyond the actual gift event. There are many forms of business incentives; the Service Monkeys have highlighted three of their favorites.

Monkey Incentive 1: The Cartoon Postcard

The cartoon postcard is a time management tool. The cartoon postcard is an inexpensive yet effective marketing tool that is often used by dentists and physicians to remind customers of upcoming appointments or events.

The effectiveness of the cartoon postcard relies heavily on humor (in the cartoon). The postcard is the gift that keeps on giving. While it conveys specific information, for example an upcoming appointment, the postcard can also remind customers of their health management objectives.

The last and maybe not-so-obvious outcome of the cartoon postcard is that it saves time. Service agents are relieved of calling customers to set appointments, which gives them more time to focus on resolving other service inquiries.

Within the Monkey service system, the cartoon postcard is a form of communication that is viewed as non-threatening, humorous, and informal.

Postcard Attributes

- A non-evasive tool. The postcard is used as a reminder notice.
- Informational invitation. It identifies not only that the appointment is due, but that it is also necessary.
- Cost. A subtle reminder of any upcoming expenses for services rendered in the future.
- Action. It requires customers to call the provider of the service in order to make an appointment.

Monkey Incentive 2: Ongoing Promotions

Many promotions are tools designed to persuade.

Persuasion tools remind customers about the company's brand and its products. However, unless the customer is asked to respond to the promotion, the purpose of the tool becomes diminished.

The most successful persuasion tools are those that are customized to interest each specific Monkey customer type.

Monkey Incentive 3: Formal Correspondence

This is a tool that uses company letterhead to elevate the importance of brand. Targeted correspondence or letter incentives are reserved for special company events and should not be overused.

Each of the three customer types respond to correspondence incentives in different ways. Constants will usually take advantage of anniversary events and specific discounts offered once a year or on the company's birthdays. These are usually important occasions that celebrate customer loyalty.

In contrast, Hunters will pay attention to promotions and service options that represent value added. Hunters will only take advantage of promotions that offer maximized purchase opportunities. This includes percentage discounts and special gift events.

Correspondence can attract Untouchables. As a general rule, Untouchables do not respond to incentives or promotions. However, because correspondence highlights brand performance, this can offer ways to distinguish the organization. When the incentive includes factual data and a specific "call to action" message, Untouchables may respond.

Monkey Chapter Overview

- An indirect benefit of the service solution system is to introduce appropriate customer gift-giving events aimed at increasing business revenue and managing customer retention.
- Any marketing or sales incentive must be supported by sufficient, trained, and knowledgeable service agents to manage customer retention opportunities.
- The correspondence incentive is used infrequently. When correspondence is used, it introduces special and iconic events.

~ ~ ~

Chapter Seventeen

Business Responsiveness

"A useful definition of liberty is obtained only by seeking the principle of liberty in the main business of human life, that is to say, in the process by which men educate their responses and learn to control their environment."

—Walter Lippman

Monkey Reaction

Providing employee training within organizations improves service responsiveness and customer satisfaction.

Service responsiveness is dependent upon the use of tools and solutions. Examples of response tools include specific processes and established business operational systems. These tools manage inquiry flow and introduce solutions that improve service delivery. The solutions offered are designed by trained service agents in the course of resolving customer inquiries.

Service responsiveness can be regulated. As service issues are identified, adjustments can be implemented to reduce the number of future negative service incidents. A reduction of service incidents improves overall customer satisfaction and organizational efficiency.

Monkey Response Tool: Phone Systems

Phone systems cannot resolve customer inquiries; however, they can manage service flow.

Phone systems are support tools that help to reduce service delays. Customized phone systems can also be designed to allow customers to receive specific information.

The following two phone system features improve service flow.

- The automated callback. This feature reduces telephone hold times by offering customers periodic notifications. For example, "Your call is the third to be answered in the queue," or "Your call wait time will be less than two minutes."
- Call tracking until the inquiry is resolved. This feature ensures phone messages are returned and service inquiries are resolved to completion.

Monkey Response Tool: E-mail

A heavy reliance on e-mail for business communication is inefficient. There are many customers, particularly Constants, who do not view their e-mail regularly. If the matter is urgent or requires an immediate response, personal phone calls improve the overall efficiency of the solution system and elevate brand significance.

Monkey Response Tool: Phone Trees

The phone tree is a regulating communication tool.

Any phone tree that does not meet its designed objective will interrupt service flow and produce customer dissatisfaction.

When customers using phone trees are required to repeat basic information, undue frustration and service delays are created.

More Delivery Interruptions

Entering a bank during lunchtime may result in experiencing long lines, delays in service, and even worse, fewer tellers to support periods of increased customer traffic.

The question that begs to be asked is, why do service agents always take their lunches and breaks during peak inquiry times?

Although legitimate staffing issues can create service delays, a thorough understanding of business flow improves scheduling and promotes greater organizational efficiency.

The rate of inquiry resolution depends upon precise employee coverage and accurate shift scheduling. Staff scheduling is not exclusive to banks but affects other service organizations that experience peak traffic conditions. This includes grocery stores, post offices, and other retail organizations.

Monkey Staffing Rule

The Service Monkeys only have one rule related to staffing efficiency: Sufficient staff coverage is required at all times to manage service volume fluctuations.

Monkey Chapter Overview

- Employee staffing is a "managed activity" that regulates business flow.
- Employee scheduling and training impacts service delivery, customer retention, and company brand recognition.
- Time management and the distribution of service agent experience during each shift are subject to a thorough understanding of business flow.
- Employee productivity is not only concerned with the length of employment, but also with the caliber of trained service agents who can deliver comprehensive customer solutions.
- Service-seeking customers are never focused on the training and scheduling shortfalls of an organization but on the immediate resolution of their service inquiries.

~ ~ ~

Chapter Eighteen

The Best Team in Town

Webster's definition of collaboration:
"to work with another."

Service, Africa Style: The Zambia Town Hall Meeting

While on holiday in Africa, a visitor decided to stay at a tourist resort that had several restaurants. One of these restaurants was a family-style establishment.

During his visit, he decided to eat lunch at this restaurant and was pleased to experience the excellent service. He noticed that he was seated immediately and that his server was friendly, polite, and courteous. Soon after ordering his food, the meal arrived from the kitchen piping hot, and to add to his satisfaction, it was delicious.

However, at the end of the meal, when he was ready to pay the bill, his server was nowhere to be found. In fact, there appeared to be no restaurant staff anywhere.

His wait wasn't too long. Soon, his server arrived and was very apologetic. He explained that the entire shift was attending the afternoon service meeting. Because the visitor was very interested in business systems, he asked for more information. He learned that the meetings occurred frequently during the day to accommodate the various employee shifts.

The server, who happened to be wearing a very smart and visible nametag, smiled and then told the visitor that these service meetings were mandatory. Each meeting lasted approximately twenty minutes, and every server and manager was tasked with reviewing the service issues during that shift. Any potentially negative service issues were corrected to improve the overall service system at the restaurant.

The visitor was surprised to discover that every server and manager had one employment goal: to continuously improve the quality of service throughout the resort.

The visitor wanted to find out more information and met with the resort manager the next day. He was impressed to learn that every direct client organization at the resort attended daily service meetings. The resort catered to approximately 1500 guests during any one week, and maintaining a high level of service required expert coordination and collaboration. This service standard was also closely monitored by the executives at the resort.

During the rest of his stay, the visitor continued to experience high-quality service. He noticed that the meals he ordered from room service arrived within fifteen minutes, and when called, every porter, bellhop, and maid arrived at his door in even less time.

During checkout, the visitor was impressed by the efficient process, particularly when there was very little automation. Every service agent was helpful, courteous, and congenial. In fact, every employee, regardless of which department he or she worked for at the resort, appeared to be part of a cohesive team. Most important, they were all approachable, solution driven, and visibly connected by dress and behavior to an established employee culture.

Establishing Monkey Teams

The concept of teamwork was introduced in the early '80s in an effort to revitalize a dwindling business infrastructure. Many of the proponents of the teamwork concept were blue-chip companies who were focused on creating standardized business protocols within their organizations.

The Malcolm Baldridge Award was created in 1987, and offered companies the opportunity to adopt higher quality service standards in order to qualify and receive this honor.[9]

Twenty years later, most if not all of these standards are no longer practiced—the main villain being a heavy reliance on technology, which has replaced the need for creative human collaboration. The financial investment and the burden of maintaining these processes were too great, and the largest deterrent of teamwork became the cost of training.

Simply stated, in the new millennium, training expense has been replaced by technology expense. As this trend continues, any significant operational change will produce greater incidents of customer dissatisfaction because more employees will be untrained and inexperienced.

Getting On Board

The Service Monkeys believe that the cost of training is a return in investment of employee tenure, dedication, and experience.

Training also produces a vibrant company culture that improves brand identity, productivity, and customer retention.

If the business culture weakens, the organizational framework deteriorates, and this in turn impacts brand performance. Employee training therefore becomes necessary for managing brand longevity, customer retention and a higher standard of service delivery.

An indirect consequence of substituting training with an overuse of technology is the lack of creative skills required to deliver high-quality customer interactions.

The teamwork approach is therefore not focused on the organization or any collective group, but on the productive outcomes that are required to resolve a variety of broad-spectrum customer inquiries.

Teamwork Standards

Teams of employees who understand the value of the company's mission are better prepared to promote brand recognition to the customers that they serve. Therefore, a combination of teamwork and training drives all business activities, from service delivery to brand association and customer retention.

Teamwork Delivery

Brainstorming is a communication tool that supports continuous teamwork. Brainstorming should not be confused with weekly staff meetings. These are stand-alone, business enhancement sessions.

Brainstorming can be used by core employee teams of various tenure and business experience to generate creative customer inquiry solutions.

Regular and continuous team collaborations support the flow of creative business ideas throughout the organization. Team collaborations also maintain the organizational culture by encouraging employees to continuously improve the standard of service delivery.

The complexity or simplicity of brainstorming events is determined by the number and variety of inquiries that require resolution. For example, at the African resort twenty minutes per shift was sufficient time to discuss service issues and implement solutions.

One More Monkey Story: The Motivated Team

One beautiful sunny day, Larry drove his four-wheel pickup truck along a farmland road. He was feeling very happy until his truck hit a deep pothole and one of the wheels got stuck in the mud.

Larry tried to reverse, but the wheel would not dislodge from the pothole. Frustrated, he decided to find help. The area was remote, and the odds of him finding help were even more remote.

He breathed a sigh of relief when he saw a small farmhouse in the distance. When he reached the farmhouse, he knocked on the front door.

The door opened, and he was greeted by an old man with a long white beard.

"Hello!" the old man said. "How can I help you?"

Larry explained the situation and asked for help with his truck.

The old man apologized. "Sorry," he said, "I am far too old and feeble to help you move your truck."

Larry understood and thanked him. As he was about to walk away, the old man shouted for him to wait.

He said, "I have an old, blind mule in the barn. Maybe we could use the mule to pull your truck from out of the pothole."

Larry was very grateful for the offer and accepted.

The old man brought his blind mule, Thunder, from the barn. They both accompanied Larry to his truck.

The old man tied Thunder to the back of the truck. He then shouted, "Peter, pull! Samuel, pull! Donald, pull!" Finally he shouted, "Thunder, pull!"

Thunder pulled and pulled, and eventually the wheel dislodged from the pothole.

Larry felt relieved. He thanked the old man for his help. Then he said: "I am curious, sir; who were those people you were calling to, Peter, Samuel, and Donald?"

The old man smiled and said, "Thunder may be old and blind, but he always pulls harder when he believes that he is working as part of a team."

—Unknown Author

Monkey Chapter Overview

- A group or family of employees is considered the team responsible for delivering high-quality customer service standards.
- Team meetings and brainstorming sessions are designed to be short, constructive, and consistent.
- Teamwork improves service delivery by encouraging creative suggestions from the entire team.
- The purpose of brainstorming is to first gain and then deliver information, and finally to enact change whenever necessary.
- Teamwork is reinforced when smaller core teams pool ideas to solve customer inquiries.
- Teamwork is essential to improving service standards because it allows employees to participate.
- Teamwork relies on an investment in high-quality and continuous training.
- The members of any team are responsible for resolving both internal and external customer service inquiries.

~ ~ ~

Chapter Nineteen

Cultural Divides

Rome could not be conquered in a day because to be Roman was considered unique and essential to the global synergy of the times.

—Unknown Author

The established employee culture determines the value and importance of service delivery and reinforces the strength of the company's brand. If the employee culture is abandoned, then the organization will lose marketplace identity.

The only exception to these conditions is when the organization itself recognizes a need to shift business focus and establishes a new mission and employee culture.

Cultural Shifts

Employee retention reflects the company's commitment to developing an employee culture that can deliver high-quality service.

A new business trend that has de-emphasized the employee culture is the use of overseas outsourcing to manage customer service.

The consistent and regular adoption of this trend has not only negatively impacted all areas of service delivery and business flow, but also deteriorated both employee and customer retention.

Global Gaps

The United States, having its own distinct culture, produces customers who have specific service expectations. In most cases, this level of service may be far superior than anywhere else in the world and comes with predetermined customer expectations.

American business standards include social responsibility, employee equality, and service excellence. Direct service can also be measured by how much a business shows its appreciation after the customer has made a purchase.

Because foreign outsourcing is not supported by the original mission of the organization, service gaps are formed, which deteriorate the fabric of the employee culture. If it continues, this deterioration produces greater and more frequent negative service outcomes where customers will be neglected and dismissed more often.

These gap conditions have a subliminal effect that creates opportunities for customers to consider the competition when they make their next purchase.

The Road Less Traveled

When customers are forced to call service centers that are based in another country, a conflict in employee cultural mannerisms is introduced.

Foreign outsourcing also relies heavily on static technology templates for service delivery, which is considered the most inefficient tool within any service solution system.

Template Design

Static templates were invented to reduce service agent error and manage revenue performance. However, the use of the template also reduces the need for trained employees and the expense for employee training.

In addition, when templates are used, the service standard is compromised because it operates independent of the employee culture and the company mission and subsequently produces service barriers.

Culture of Origin

All service expectations are established by the company culture and dictated by customer buying influence. For example, in Western developed nations, buying power is determined by obscure factors that are far removed from the actual product or service that was originally purchased. These factors include the ethnicity of the buyer and even the influence of women as a specific buying group. In certain Western global markets, women may have more buying influence than other consumer groups, and they also can dictate the course of service delivery.

In comparison, within developing countries, women often have less buying power because they have less influence within the culture.

Monkey Secrets

Overseas outsourcing has also created serious privacy concerns. In recent years, insufficient security measures have caused personal data of customers to be lost or compromised. Where this information was once managed by companies in the culture of origin, the expanded use of technology has moved private and personal consumer information to overseas vendors who have less cultural connection with the service source and offer this service for a fee. As this practice continues, it exposes customers to unmanageable and unknown risks.

In a recent example, the British government experienced several serious security breaches that involved the leaking of personal consumer information. In 2007 and 2008, the loss of unencrypted files exposed the private information of millions of people.[10]

In another incident, 3,000 blank British passports were stolen when they were being transported to another location. As incidents, these were random acts, but they serve to illustrate the inefficiencies that exist when outsourcing relies on untested practices.[11]

Monkey Chapter Overview

- Foreign cultural factors impact the flow of service delivery.
- Template customer service is both inadequate and ineffective when used as a cultural bridging device.
- Service delivery is at its most efficient when it is delivered by the culture of origin.
- Company culture is influenced by service expectations that are created by specific consumer groups who have varying buying influence.
- Outsourcing to developing nations is unable to bridge cultural gaps, even when static service templates are used to artificially create the service environment.
- Cultural gaps produce customer frustration, inhibit service flow, and denigrate company brand. These unmonitored outcomes impact customer retention.
- Overseas outsourcing of customer service can produce both cultural frustration and unexpected security breaches.

~ ~ ~

Chapter Twenty

Service Technology

"Customer service is a series of activities designed to enhance the level of customer satisfaction—that is, the feeling that a product or service has met the customer's expectation."

—Turban

Monkey Managed

Providing service is always optional but advisable. If service is offered, the quality of service determines all customer satisfaction outcomes.

Service is not considered effective when it is offered for the sake of appearances.

Tech Monkeys

Monkey service builds human activity systems that are supported by technology but never managed by technology.

Technology-driven service systems are incapable of overriding culture, tradition, and social values. Any service system that is supported by technology is only as effective as the human ingenuity that created it.

In order to maintain service standards, technology must be upgraded to meet the demands of a changing business and service environment.

Phone Tree Management

Phone trees are a service technology tool. Phone systems that utilize phone trees rely on predetermined prompts to navigate call traffic.

Having prompts requires customers to "learn" how to use the phone tree in order to activate the appropriate solutions for their specific service inquiries.

Technology History

The phone tree is not a high communication interface; it is a tool within a tool, which serves two activities. First, the phone tree manages call volume, and second, it provides information, for example customer account history and other generic details.

Automation Effectiveness

The phone tree or automated phone systems (APS) offer customers basic information. This information is inferior to trained service support because the information is static, not customized, and must be updated frequently to insure accuracy.

Within Monkey service systems, the APS is managed and monitored by the organization that created it. Upgrading the APS becomes critical to delivering a higher standard of service.

An example of an efficient, streamlined APS is the automated jury selection system, which monitors juror attendance. These systems are usually available twenty-four hours a day and may or may not be connected to live service support. These systems provide jurors with specific information about the duration of their jury service, court reporting times, and other schedules that may change daily. Based on the sensitive nature of this information, in order to be reliable this type of APS must be updated regularly.

Monkey Chapter Overview

- Technology never replaces trained service agent support because it cannot offer customized solutions.
- Voice mail and answering systems may be required based on high call volume; however, these conditions infer the absence of both sufficient and trained service agents.
- The phone tree is a technology tool and viewed as one component of the entire solution service system.
- "Automated" and "live" service options are always independent of one another.

~ ~ ~

Chapter Twenty-One

Important Versus Necessary

Customer service is important because it connects the employee culture with the mission statement and purpose of the organization. Within Monkey service systems, customers represent long-term loyalty and brand appreciation. Maintaining a business advantage requires retaining customers who have purchased products and are already familiar with the brand.

Proper design and implementation of the entire service system depends upon predetermined standards of quality. These standards are designed to manage brand recognition in the general product marketplace. They also deter competition, particularly during economic recessions and periods of reduced product research and development. Deterring competition retains more customers, which reduces future marketing and advertising expenses.

Understanding the various customer types that buy products and services can serve to manage overall costs and justify the expense of high-quality employee training.

Each customer type in the service hourglass controls the number of revenue-generating promotions and incentives that are offered by the organization.

Losing even one customer is unacceptable because this represents a loss of future marketing and sales revenue. This includes the marketing expense that is required to bring customers to the product and any future revenue that is lost when an existing customer buys from the competition.

Trained employees support business longevity. Important employees represent opportunities to increase revenue, generate future sales, and manage market share by elevating brand integrity.

The foundation for the employee culture is established with high-quality service training, which creates direction and greater organization-wide participation.

Necessary behaviors are always secondary within the organizational structure. The necessary employee is transient; the important employee belongs to the important team that generates important service solutions and manages customer retention.

A necessary business is represented by the number of support tools, peripheral technologies, and company processes required for it to function. Necessary relates to the mechanical operation and any related expenses, and not to the employee culture or brand that are important to building business growth and company longevity.

Application of the necessary-versus-important principle affects every aspect of organizational flow, from employee productivity to the relevance of marketing incentives.

When properly monitored, important and necessary ideals manage the quality standards of the entire service delivery system. Important and necessary directs the business focus toward managing customer retention, understanding service flow, and delivering high-quality service to every customer that the organization serves.

~ ~ ~

Also Available from Bright Performance:

Health & Weight Loss
Companion,
Everyday Journal

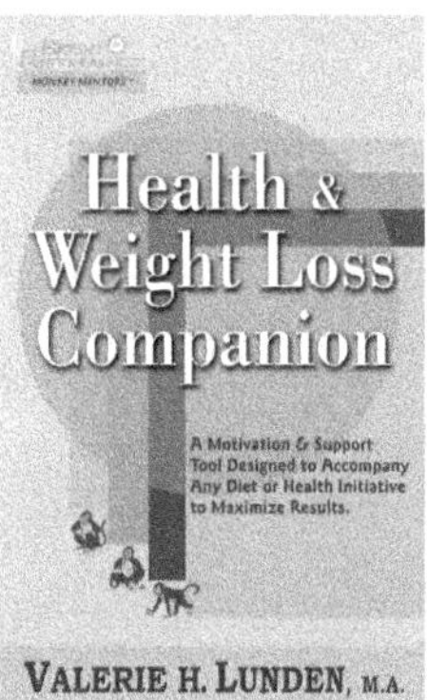

Health & Weight Loss
Companion

Four disk CD Set

To purchase, visit BrightPerformance.com

Monkey Terms

EBI:	Exceptional buying influence.
Reverse Economy:	A shift in buying dependency.
Solution Utility:	A service system that adopts consistent and continuous training methods.
Continuous Civility:	The relationship between company brand and the customer within the general product marketplace.
Service Tag Team:	The entire service solution system, which may include the entire organization as a combination of service groups.

Endnotes

1. "Gene similarity." Frequently asked questions: Chimpanzee and Human Communication Institute, 2004. Accessible at: http://www.cwu.edu/cwuchci:faq.html.
2. Mary Ellen Podmolik and Michael Oneal, "Parents cast wary eye toward toy chests," Chicago Tribune (August 10, 2007). Accessible at: http://www.chicagotribune.com/news/nationworld/chi-fri_toys0810aug10,0,2358406.story.
3. Associated Press, "104 deaths reported in pet food recall," New York Times (March 28, 2007). Accessible at: http://www.nytimes.com/2007/03/28/science/28brfs-pet.html?_r=1&ex=1176264000&en=8ee0fb91fd221e4b&ei=5070&oref=slogin.
4. Associated Press, "Cadbury: Melamine found in Chinese-made chocolates," International Herald Tribune (September 29, 2008). Accessible at: http://www.iht.com/articles/ap/2008/09/29/asia/AS-Asia-Tainted-Milk.php.
5. Jeffrey Abrahams, "Star Trek Mission Statement," The Mission Statement Book. Accessible at: http://books.google.com/books?id=E1zIw32gWoC&dq=Mission+statement+star+trek&pg=PP1&ots=ayKUj2KeIc&source=in&sig=ECDnvcBhgiwLFU0tx6_ZvDdbwpw&hl=en&sa=X&oi=book_result&resnum=11&ct=result.
6. "Leadership through Quality," http://www.quality.nist.gov/Xerox_89.htm.

7. FedEx Mission Statement, http://officeproducts.fedexkinkos.com/ce/shop/bulletin.b_view?title=answers_mission_guarantee.
8. "Detroit tops nation in poverty census – Chapter Seven," http://www-personal.umich.edu/~gmarkus/montemurri.htm. John Flesher, "Incomes rise in Michigan, but more in poverty," Cranes Detroit Business. Accessible at: www.crainsdetroit.com/article/20080826/REG/16549179/1069/-/-/incomes-rise-in-michigan-but-more-in-poverty.
9. Malcolm Baldridge Award, http://www.quality.nist.gov/Improvement_Act.htm.
10. John F. Burns, "British inmates' private data is lost in latest government security breach," New York Times (August 22, 2008). Accessible at: http://www.nytimes.com/2008/08/23/world/europe/23britain.html?fta=y.
11. Christopher Pledger, "Stolen passports 'worth up to £5 million'," The Times (July 29, 2008). Accessible at: http://www.timesonline.co.uk/tol/news/uk/crime/article4420850.ece.

References & Notes

Introduction
Quote: Peter Drucker

Chapter One—Fairy Tale Manufacturing
Quote: Albert Schweitzer
2. (1-1) Illustrates Unemployment Population Survey:
Source: Bureau of Labor Statistics, Current Population Survey
http://data.bls.gov/PDQ/servlet/SurveyOutputServlet?request_action=wh&graph_name=LN_cpsbref3
3. (1-2) Decline of New Orders - Manufacturing
Source: U.S. Census Bureau
http://www.census.gov/briefrm/esbr/www/esbr022.html
4. (1-3) U.S International Trade in Goods & Services
Source: U.S Census Bureaus
http://www.census.gov/briefrm/esbr/www/esbr042.html

Chapter Two—Monkey Service
Quote: Mahatma Gandhi
(2) "Gene similarity." Frequently asked questions: Chimpanzee and Human Communication Institute, 2004. Accessible at: http://www.cwu.edu/cwuchci:faq.html.

Chapter Four—Monkey Training
Quote: Ann Radcliffe, The Mysteries of Udolpho, 1764

Chapter Five—Monkey Competition
Webster definition : To Evolve
Source: Webster's Vest Pocket Dictionary. Merriam Webster 1981

(5a) Parents cast wary eye toward toy chests

By Mary Ellen Podmolik and Michael Oneal, Chicago Tribune; Mary Ellen Podmolik is a freelance writer. Michael Oneal is a staff reporter August 10, 2007
http://www.chicagotribune.com/news/nationworld/chi-fri_toys0810aug10,0,2358406.story

(5b) 104 Deaths Reported in Pet Food Recall
By The Associated press - Published: March 28, 2007
http://www.nytimes.com/2007/03/28/science/28brfs-pet.html?_r=1&ex=1176264000&en=8ee0fb91fd221e4b&ei=5070&oref=slogin
(5c) International Herald Tribune: Cadbury: Melamine found in Chinese-made chocolates
The Associated Press - Published: September 29, 2008
http://www.iht.com/articles/ap/2008/09/29/asia/AS-Asia-Tainted-Milk.php

Chapter Six—Monkey Migration
Webster definition : To Serve
Source: Webster's Vest Pocket Dictionary. Merriam Webster 1981

Chapter Seven—Monkey Solution Systems
Webster definition : Customer
Source: Webster's Vest Pocket Dictionary. Merriam Webster 1981

Chapter Eight—The Mission
Quote: Robert Kiyosaki
(8a) Star Trek Mission Statement
The Mission Statement Book By Jeffrey Abrahams
http://books.google.com/books?id=E1zIw32gWoC&dq=Mission+statement+star+trek&pg=PP1&ots=ayKUj2KeIc&source=in&sig=ECDnvcBhgiwLFU0tx6_ZvDdbwpw&hl=en&sa=X&oi=book_result&resnum=11&ct=result

(8b) Leadership Through Quality
http://www.quality.nist.gov/Xerox_89.htm
(8c) FedEx Mission Statement
http://officeproducts.fedexkinkos.com/ce/shop/bulletin.b_view?title=answers_mission_guarantee

Chapter Ten—Why the Customer Always Wins
Quote:Norman Cousins
(10a) Detroit tops nation in poverty census – Chapter Seven
http://www-personal.umich.edu/~gmarkus/montemurri.htm
(10b) Cranes Detroit Business - Incomes rise in Michigan, but more in poverty By John Flesher
www.crainsdetroit.com/article/20080826/REG/16549179/1069/-/-/incomes-rise-in-michigan-but-more-in-poverty
(10c) A hypothetical example of this buying dynamics

Chapter Eleven—Service Templates- The Destroyers!
Quote: Steven Pressfield, The War of Art

Chapter Twelve—You are Going to Transfer Me Where?
Quote: Robert Kiyosaki

Chapter Thirteen—Monkey's Web Solutions
Quote: Robert Kiyosaki

Chapter Fourteen—Solutions in Motion
Quote: Paul W. Swets, The Art of Talking so that People will Listen.

Chapter Fifteen—Monkey Follow Through
Quote: Norman Vincent Peale

Chapter Sixteen—Gift Days
Quote: Francois Marie Arouet (Voltaire)

Chapter Seventeen—Responsiveness
Quote: Walter Lippman

Chapter Eighteen—The Best Team in Town
(18a) Malcom Baldridge Award
http://www.quality.nist.gov/Improvement_Act.htm

Chapter Nineteen—The Cultural Divide
(19a) British Inmates' Private Data Is Lost in Latest Government Security Breach
The New York Times. Published: August 22, 2008 By JOHN F. BURNS
http://www.nytimes.com/2008/08/23/world/europe/23britain.html?fta=y

(19b) Stolen passports 'worth up to £5 million'
From Times Online July 29, 2008, Christopher Pledger /The Times
http://www.timesonline.co.uk/tol/news/uk/crime/article4420850.ece

Chapter Twenty—Technology Phone Trees
Quote: Turban et al, 2002
http://en.wikipedia.org/wiki/Customer_service

Bibliography

Carnegie, Dale. How to Win Friends & Influence People. New York: Pocket Books, 1982.

Collins, Jim. Good to Great. New York: Harper Collins, 2001.

Covey, Stephen R. The 7 Habits of Highly Effective People. New York: First Fireside Edition, 1990.

Gladwell, Malcolm. Blink. New York: Time Warner Book Group, 2005.

Hawkins, David R. Power VS. Force. California: Hay House, 2002.

Pressfield, Steven. The War of Art. New York: Warner Books, 2002.

Singer, Blair. The ABC's of Building a Business Team that Wins. New York: Time Warner Book Group, 2004.

Stanley, Thomas J. and William D. Danko. The Millionaire Next Door. New York: Pocket Books, 2000.

Swets, Paul W. The Art of Talking So That People Will Listen. New York: First Fireside Edition, 1992.